THE WHOLE YOU
Spirit

THE WHOLE YOU

A GUIDE TO LIFE

Spirit

by Jeannie Kim

AN
APPLE
PAPERBACK

SCHOLASTIC INC.

NEW YORK TORONTO LONDON AUCKLAND SYDNEY
MEXICO CITY NEW DELHI HONG KONG BUENOS AIRES

ISBN 0-439-40463-0

12 11 10 9 8 7 6 5   3 4 5 6 7/0

Printed in the U.S.A.   40

First printing, September 2002

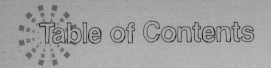
Table of Contents

Acknowledgments

I am forever grateful to:

David Levithan, editor extraordinaire and all-around amazing guy, and Anica Rissi, whose stellar suggestions helped take this book to the next level.

Muney, Steven, Lucey, and (especially!) Izzy Rivers, who fed me, let me take over their house, and inspired many pieces of *The Whole You;* and Shauna, Sydney, and Christina, who bared their souls over pizza and Popsicles.

Fred Seibert, Parker Reilly, Anne Marie DeLuca, and the kids at Secret Goldfish who shared the insides of their heads with a total stranger.

All the kids whose stories appear throughout this book.

My family, who shaped my spirit.

And Adam, who keeps me whole.

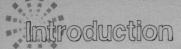

Introduction
The Whole You:
Getting to Know You

Welcome to **The Whole You!** Right now, you're at an exciting point in life. You're learning all about the world, and you're learning all about yourself, too. This is your road map on that journey of exploration.

What's spirit?

When you hear the word "spirit," you might think of stuff like ghosts. But what we're talking about here is *your* spirit. Spirit is a key part of **The Whole You**. It means self-knowledge, self-confidence, values, emotions, inner peace — **all the stuff that's deep inside you and is the core of who you are.** When your spirit is strong, you feel more whole.

To connect with your spirit, we'll be delving into all the different parts of your inner self and learning about how all of those different parts make up the whole you. Most important, not only will we learn about the person you already are, **we'll also explore the person you dream of being and the person you could**

"The spirit is
the true self."
— Cicero
Roman orator
and statesman

be someday. See, your spirit is still growing and learning, day by day. You're going to keep adding to the person you are for years and years. Now is a great time to have fun trying on different possibilities and learning about all the exciting choices you have.

What is The Whole You?

Right now, a whole world of options is opening up around you. Whether you know it or not, your life is full of amazing opportunities, and you yourself are overflowing with all kinds of potential and personality and talent that you've only just begun to discover. **The Whole You** is based on the idea that it's important to explore all of your options and **grab every chance to learn something new about the incredible, exciting whole that is you.**

Everything in your life contributes to the whole you, from the values you hold and the friends you make to the way you take care of your body. And all of those things can help you discover the person you are and the person you want to be. Why is this important? **The more you know about yourself, the easier it will be to make the right choices about your life** — choices that keep you whole and happy, instead of making you feel like you're torn apart.

Because **The Whole You** is about discovering YOU, you get to decide the path you take. That means I won't be giving you a bossy set of instructions on the best way to live your life or a boring list of ten steps to success. You're creating *yourself* — there's no magic formula for that. I'll also never tell you that there are things wrong with you that need to be fixed. That's because every single person who reads **The Whole You** is different and cool in her or his own way.

I'm not a teacher or a psychologist. But as a writer and editor for teen magazines, I've spent tons of time talking to kids from all over the world about the stuff that matters most to them. And, of course, I've also been through a lot of the same kinds of struggles, questions, good times, and bad times that you're going through right now. So throughout **The Whole You**, I'll share stories from my own experiences as well as stories from other kids. (You'll see those marked with a ✓ ***REALITY CHECK*** icon.) Everything in **The Whole You** is based on real life — not on some theory about how kids are supposed to be.

Finally, and most important, **The Whole You** is supposed to be fun. You'll find plenty of hands-on activities to get you thinking and playing — and, I hope, exploring the whole you!

How to use this book

Like I said before, **The Whole You** is *your* journey — so you're the one who decides the way you want to use it. Every chapter of **The Whole You** is packed with plenty of activities and exercises. You can do most of the ➤ *WRITE IT!* exercises right in the book (or in a separate notebook, if you don't like writing in your books). ☀ *WORK IT!* activities are more hands-on; you might find it fun to do some of them with friends.

You don't have to do every single activity — just do the ones that appeal to you and save the rest for later. You don't have to start reading at the beginning of the book and work straight through to the end, either. (After all, learning about yourself doesn't happen in a straight, orderly line.) In fact, I encourage you to skip around — to help you do that, I've included ✿ *LINKS* in each chapter to point you to other chapters, other books in **The Whole You,** even Web sites and other resources that might interest you. You might feel like skimming through one chapter, then spending hours on another chapter, doing every single activity — it's up to you.

Enough talk. You've got cool, creative, fascinating corners of you that are just waiting to be explored. So let's get started!

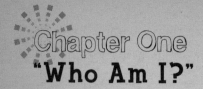

Chapter One
"Who Am I?"

Who are you?

If someone asked you that question, what would pop into your head? Your name might be first, along with what you look like, where you go to school, or what you like to do. But the question "Who are you?" goes deeper than that. It's about what kind of person you are and how you choose to describe yourself.

>WRITE IT! Make a list of at least twenty one- or two-word phrases that describe you. For example, I could write, "I am a writer, a violinist, a secret slob, a romantic, a good friend, a decent cook, a bookworm, a shoe addict . . ." etc. Use these examples to inspire your list:

I am . . .

a student	a boy	an activist
a math lover	a girl	a soccer star
a trumpet player	a hard worker	a pessimist
a goofy dancer	a TV addict	a leader

6

a cat lover   a fashion queen   a chocoholic

a computer whiz   a brain   a future DJ

a *Buffy* fan   a dreamer   a class clown

a neat freak   a vegetarian   a bad liar

I am . . .

a student	activist	a tomboy
a girl	a piano player	earring addict
a truth lover	boy lover	TV lover
shoe addict	a messy person	animal lover
hard worker	a good liar ?	
dreamer	shopoholic	
chocoholic	bookworm	
a leader	good friend	

Now make a list of at least twenty adjectives
that describe you. Write down everything that
comes into your head, whether it's positive or
negative. Use these examples to inspire you:

I am . . .

silly   creative   gullible

organized   lazy   kind

athletic   strong   funny

tall   messy   shy

cheerful	smart	generous
brave	quiet	lucky
klutzy	spacey	sneaky
gossipy	interesting	flexible

I am . . .

_____	_____	_____
_____	_____	_____
_____	_____	_____
_____	_____	_____
_____	_____	_____
_____	_____	_____
_____	_____	_____
_____	_____	_____

Take a look at both of your lists. What do these phrases and adjectives mean to you? Which are you proud of? Which do you wish you could change? Why?

Some things on your lists take up more space in the whole you than others. For example, "I am a soccer star" might be a very significant part of your life, while "I am sneaky" isn't something that comes up as often. But **all of your parts are important, big or small.** Discovering those little parts is just as important as exploring the bigger parts, since it's the unique combination of big and little parts that makes the whole you.

You might find that some things on your lists seem to contradict each other. For example, I would put "I am a hard worker" on my first list, and "I am lazy" on my second list, which doesn't make much sense at first. But the truth is that sometimes I'm a hard worker (like when I'm writing something fun) and sometimes I'm a little lazy (like when I'm tired or when it's time to do the dishes!). Both of those things are part of me.

You see, **it takes more than a list of labels to describe who you really are.** Making a list is a start, but it's also important to see how the things on your list are related. Just saying "I am a hard worker" doesn't describe me, and neither does "I am lazy." They each represent a piece of me, but to see my whole self, I need to see how the pieces fit together. It's like a collage — each piece or image makes a statement on its own, and some of them might not seem like they go together. But when you put them all next to one another, they work together to create a whole new image or idea — and

> **"I am just too much."**
> — Bette Davis, actress, when asked to describe herself in five words

each new piece you add gives the collage a whole new meaning.

So to really understand the whole you, let's start looking at how all the bits and pieces of your life fit together. Everything on those lists describes a part of you. Some things are good, some things may be not so good, some things contradict one another. But *all* of them are important to the whole you, and you wouldn't be the same person without them.

☛"WRITE IT!" Pick five adjectives from your list. For each one, write one or two sentences explaining why this adjective describes you. (For example, if you wrote, "I am cheerful," you could say, "I always look on the bright side of things. My nickname is Smiley because I always have a smile on my face.")

Adjective #1: _____

Why it describes me: _____

_____

Adjective #2: _____

Why it describes me: _____

_____

Adjective #3: _____

Why it describes me: _____

_____

Adjective #4: _____

Why it describes me: _____

_____

Adjective #5: _____

Why it describes me: _____

_____

WRITE IT! Pick any two phrases from your first list. (Close your eyes and point to the list to pick two totally at random.) Can you think of a way that they're related? From my list, if I picked "I am a romantic" and "I am a book- worm," I would say that they're related be- cause I like serious books *and* I secretly love cheesy romance novels and love stories of all kinds. If I picked "I am a violinist" and "I am a decent cook," I would say that they're related because they are both creative activities that you have to practice doing if you want to get better at them. How are yours related?

_____

_____

_____

◗"WRITE IT!" Are there two things on your lists that contradict each other? Explain why they are both true.

_____

_____

_____

✸"WORK IT!" Create a collage that represents *you*. Collect images, words, and objects that relate to the lists you just made — a picture of a soccer ball, a chocolate wrapper, an old paintbrush, a piece of sheet music, words cut out of magazines, photos of your favorite places. Try to include at least one image, word, or object for each thing on your lists. Arrange them on a large piece of paper or poster board. Make sure the paper is big enough that there's lots of blank space around the edges of your collage, so it can grow as you discover new things about yourself that you think should be added.

> "Resolve to be thyself; and know, that he who finds himself, loses his misery."
> — Matthew Arnold, poet and essayist

Another important part of knowing yourself is discovering your likes, dislikes, and opinions. Okay, most people like pizza, and it's safe to say that almost everyone dislikes getting hurt, but you're also developing a unique set of opinions that's all your own. No one else sees the world quite like you do, so no one else feels exactly the way you do about everything — not even your closest

> "The one self-knowledge worth having is to know one's own mind."
> — F.H. Bradley, philosopher

friends. As you explore and learn more about yourself and the world around you, you'll uncover more and more opinions and maybe change your mind about some of the ones you have now.

"WRITE IT!" List 10 things you really like. Try to think of stuff that says *you* — so don't

13

write "animals," write "big, friendly dogs." Don't write "summer vacation," write "hanging out at the pool all summer" or "going camping with my family." Don't write "pizza," write "pizza with pineapple."

_____

_____

_____

_____

_____

_____

_____

_____

_____

_____

Now list 10 things you really dislike.

_____

_____

_____

_____

_____

_____

_____

_____

_____

_____

Have a friend make the same lists, and then compare your lists. Is there anything on your friend's list that seems crazy to you or anything on your list that seems crazy to your friend? (It's good if they're not identical — it means you each definitely have a mind of your own!)

Okay, so you've started to put the pieces together, and you're starting to see a picture of yourself. What do you see, and how do you feel about it? That's really up to you. You get to choose how you see yourself. Suppose you wrote, "I am a dreamer" above. You decide exactly what that means. Maybe it means, "I am ambitious and always thinking about the future."

✂*LINKS*

Turn to Chapter 2 (What Matters to You — and Why It Matters) and Chapter 5 (Accepting Yourself — and Everyone Else) for more on respecting and accepting other people's opinions, even when you disagree. Chapter 2 also has more on knowing your own mind and sticking to it, especially when it comes to choosing the values you live by.

15

Maybe it means, "I am creative and adventurous." Maybe it means, "I am totally spacey!" You also decide how you feel about it. Is it something you're proud of, something you want to change, or something you're happy to just let be? And you decide whether you think it's a big part of your picture or just a little corner. (You decide whether it's on your list at all!)

I used to be mortified by the fact that I was terrible at any sport that involved a ball — softball, tennis, basketball, kickball — you name it, I stunk. Gym class was so humiliating — I can't even count the number of times I got beaned in the head by a volleyball. I tortured myself about it for a few years, but eventually, I figured out that there were other things I could do — hey, running and swimming don't involve balls at all! — and more important, I realized that being a great tennis player wasn't that essential to me in the big picture. I still stink at ball sports, and I probably always will — but it's okay, because I decided that it's just a quirky, kind of funny, very small part of me.

> ✂ *LINKS*
> Turn to *Body and Mind*, Chapter 3 (Working It), for activities that explore *your* athletic strengths.

WRITE IT! Write a description of yourself (two or three sentences) that is totally glowing and positive.

_____
_____
_____
_____

LINKS Check out *Creativity*, Chapter 2 (Performing the Arts), for ideas for creative ways to "try on" different kinds of personalities.

Next, write one that's totally negative.

_____
_____
_____
_____

Now, write one that's funny.

_____
_____
_____
_____

Do these descriptions sound like they're talking about the same person? They're all you — but you decide which one you believe. (Maybe

✂️ *LINKS*
Read more about taking pride in all your parts in Chapter 5 (Accepting Yourself — and Everyone Else). Chapter 6 (Peace Out!) has more on taking a positive attitude toward life.

you'll choose bits and pieces from each!)

How others see you

You get to choose how you see yourself, but lots of times, you don't get to choose how others see you.

✔️ *REALITY CHECK* Shauna loves being a cheerleader at her school, but her big complaint is that "Everyone thinks we're ditsy because we're cheerleaders." Kate says that people have often thought of her as "that geek girl," because she's into *Star Trek* and used to dress less fashionably.

Chelsye remembers that even though other people thought she was creative and funny, she didn't always see it herself. "I was too busy being modest to accept compliments," she says. But in time, the compliments she got helped her to see herself as creative, too.

Sometimes, the difference between how others see you and how you see yourself can be good for the whole you. Other people can help you see parts of yourself that you've never seen before — that's what happened for Chelsye. And the more you explore those parts, the better you know yourself.

Other times, the way others see you can be damaging. That often happens when people put labels on you. The labels could be good *or* bad — for example, you could be labeled as athletic, or smart, or klutzy, or pretty, or nerdy. But **if someone labels you, they're only seeing one part of you.** They put you in a box based on one part of your personality, or because of how you look, or who your friends are because it's easier than seeing the whole you.

✔ ***REALITY CHECK*** Sydney always gets labeled because she's thin: "People tell me, 'You're too skinny,'" she says. "In fifth grade, someone actually called me anorexic. That makes me so mad." Those people didn't bother to find out whether their label was true or not — they just saw that Sydney was thin and made up their minds without even knowing her.

Maeve has had lots of people make negative assumptions about her based on her nonconformist, punk look. "People are often surprised to find out that I'm smart, athletic, and fairly popular. Once, I was attending a meeting at my town hall for a community service group I'm involved in, and I was mistaken for someone being prosecuted in the town court."

Shauna had the experience of being labeled by a teacher: "My math teacher thought I just liked to clown around because I had a few friends in class who I'd talk to all the time. So he never took me seriously." Every time Shauna raised her hand to answer a question, her teacher would roll his eyes and act like she couldn't possibly know the answer.

WRITE IT! Look back at the lists of phrases and adjectives you made earlier. Are any of them labels that someone else gave you? Pick one and write on a separate piece of paper about how you got that label. Did something happen to make people see you that way? Is it a positive or a negative label? How do you feel about it?

It's so frustrating to be labeled but, unfortunately, you can't make everyone stop labeling you. You *can* try not to let their labels decide how you see yourself. That's important, because **if you get stuck in a box that someone else put you in, it interferes with your exploring your whole self.** For example, suppose you're a cheerleader and people assume you're ditsy, or you're an athlete and people assume you're a meathead, or you get good grades and people assume you're only interested in studying. If you let that label affect how you see yourself, you might start to believe the label, and you might not try to be anything different or explore the parts of you that *are* different.

That goes for positive labels, too. It might not *sound* so harsh to be labeled as "the smart one" or "the pretty one" — in fact, it sounds like a compliment. But no matter how positive a label seems, it still limits you, because it doesn't recognize any of the other parts of the whole you. Thinking of yourself as just "the smart one," "the pretty one," or "the basketball star" might keep you from delving into your secret passion for

✂ ***LINKS*** Turn to *Creativity* for more on the importance of trying new things — and making lots of mistakes!

punk rock or showing off your wicked sense of humor. And it puts pressure on you, too, because when you start to feel like you *always* have to be "the basketball star" or "the smart one," there's no room left for making mistakes.

✔ ***REALITY CHECK*** "I've been an A student all through school," says Amy, "so a lot of times people would think that I lived the perfect life — that school and stuff just came so easily to me. But in reality, it was so hard. I was under so much stress, and I couldn't tell anyone. I felt like the real me was a big letdown — I wasn't this fantastically intelligent being that everyone thought I was."

Accepting the labels that other people put on you limits your possibilities. That's true whether the labels are based on how you look, how you act, what culture you come from, what you used to be like when you were little, or any of the million other things people use to label one another.

How do you bust out of the box? First, the better you get to know the whole you from the inside, the easier it will be to ignore those labels from people on the outside. Another thing you can do is to look for friends and other people who are willing to see more of the whole you. When you and the people you care about recognize the value of the true you, it gives you the strength to show your real self to the world — and not care what anyone else thinks.

✓ *REALITY CHECK* Shauna knew she was more than the clown her math teacher thought she was. But it still felt good proving him wrong. "One day there was a really complicated problem that no one else could answer — and I answered it," she says. "He took me seriously after that!"

For Kate, getting rid of the "geek" label was just a matter of time. "I never tried to change myself or my image," she says. "I just kind of rode it out. I met some nice people who are still my friends today, and as my classmates and I matured, I somehow shed the 'geek' label." The important thing, though, is that Kate knew herself well enough not to let a label affect the way she felt about herself. In fact,

✂***LINKS***
**There's more
about dealing
with how others
see you in**
*Friends and
Family,* **Chapter
3 (Fitting In).**

she's taken that label and turned it into something positive: "I still love computers and sci-fi," she says. "I've simply learned to embrace my geeki-ness as a positive part of myself. I'm proud of being geeky!"

☀***WORK IT!*** Take a shoe box and decorate the outside with pictures, words, and things that represent how other people see you on the outside. Then decorate the inside of the box to represent how you see yourself on the inside.

☀***WORK IT!*** Make a list of ten to fifteen adjectives that describe your best friend, and have your friend do the same for you. Trade lists, and see what the other wrote. Do you agree with the way your friend sees you? Is there anything on your friend's list that sur-prises you or seems wrong? Talk it over.

Changes

You'll never be finished getting to know yourself. Each day, you continue to grow. Some parts of your personality are still forming; others are hidden away, waiting for you to find them. You'll discover them little by little for years to come. You'll try on new identities and decide whether they fit you or not. It's all part of the journey.

> "A finished person is a boring person."
> — Anna Quindlen, author

Not only will you find new pieces, some of the ones you already know about will change — sometimes a little, sometimes a lot. You see, while there's a core part of you that stays constant, parts of your personality are constantly evolving. In fact, you'll keep changing your whole life! (How boring would it be if you were exactly the same at age thirty as you are now?) It could be something as little as going from hating spinach to loving it (that happened to me!) or something as big as changing your mind about the kinds of friends you want to hang out with. Even the parts you already know about can evolve. I started playing the violin when I was four, but I didn't discover that I could play rock music on it until I was in my twenties. All of these changes add something to the whole you.

> **Did you know?** Researchers say that our brains go through a huge reorganization starting at around age eleven, and they continue to grow and develop all through the teen years.

✓ **"REALITY CHECK"** Andrew, now in high school, has found his interests changing. "I've discovered what kinds of books I like, mostly biographies, and what I like to read about. I have only recently found my tastes for law and history."

Kate says, "The greatest change I've seen in myself is my character strength. I think getting picked on when I was younger strengthened my character and self-assurance and, most important, my independence."

"I feel like my core has stayed the same throughout my whole life," says Marianne, "but I've learned so much that I couldn't help but become a new version of myself."

Chelsye puts it this way: "I dress a lot differently, and I think more positively, but I am still Chelsye."

You might not know these changes are happening at the time — just like you can't feel yourself growing taller. But it's nice to look back once in a while at what you used to be like and compare it to what you're like today. Remember, the old you is part of the whole you, too!

LINKS
You'll find out more about the changes going on in your mind *and* your body in *Body and Mind.*

WORK IT! Create a photo time line of yourself, from when you were a baby to today. Make sure to include at least one photo from every year of your life. For each photo, write a little description of yourself at that age: what you were like, what you liked to do, something important that happened to you, or anything else you want to include.

"A self is, by its very essence, a being with a past."
— Josiah Royce, philosopher

WRITE IT! On a separate piece of paper, write a letter to yourself at age eighteen. Tell your future self all about what you're like now, and ask eighteen-year-old you questions about what your life will be like then. Put the letter in a safe place, so you'll be sure to read it when you're eighteen!

WRITE IT! On a separate piece of paper, write an imaginary letter from yourself at age eighteen to yourself now. What kind of advice do you think you'd give yourself? What does your eighteen-year-old self think about the things you're going through now?

✳ *WORK IT!* Make a time capsule. Take a box or other sturdy container (try a cookie tin, a big jar, or a large Tupperware container) and fill it with things that represent your life now. You might include pictures of yourself and your friends and family, a mix of your favorite songs, a report you wrote for school, a list of your favorite Web sites, souvenirs from a vacation you took, a letter to the future you — anything you want! If you like, decorate the inside and outside of your time capsule. Seal it up with tape.

Decide when you want to open the time capsule (at least four or five years is good), and write "TIME CAP-

⚜ *LINKS*
In 2001, The *New York Times* Capsule was installed outside the American Museum of Natural History in New York. This time capsule is supposed to be opened in the year 3000. To see what's in it, go to the Museum's Web site at *http://www.amnh.org/exhibitions/timescapsule/contents.html*

SULE: DO NOT OPEN UNTIL [date to be opened]" on the outside. Put it in a safe place, like your attic or basement. If it's okay with your parents, you could bury it in your yard — just be sure to seal it in a plastic bag first and write down where you buried it so you don't forget!

Chapter Two

What Matters to You – and Why It Matters

What are values?

Politicians are always talking about values on TV. Parents fight about what kind of values should be taught in school. So what do we mean when we talk about "values" in **The Whole You? Your values are the standards, morals, and beliefs that you live your life by.** They help you decide what's right and what's wrong, and they influence what's important to you. They show you how to act, how to treat other people, and how to be a good member of your community.

> ✔ ***REALITY CHECK*** For Christina, it's important to treat others the way she would want to be treated. "You have to walk a mile in their shoes," she says. To Izzy, doing well in school is an important value. One of Sydney's biggest values is, "You shouldn't abuse animals." And for Shauna, believing in God is central to her values.

Andrew's personal motto is, "Work hard." For Chelsye, it's important to respect her mother: "She is tolerant and generous, and she respects me and my privacy, so I respect her." Jeff believes in being committed to any group you're a member of, "whether it's a team, band, or other group," and in treating all people equally.

Why are values important to the whole you? **Part of learning about yourself as a whole person is discovering what you believe in.** Your values are a fundamental part of who you are, and they affect every part of your life. By exploring different values and learning about which ones feel right to you, you'll better discover the whole you. You'll also be more able to make choices that fit in with the kind of person you want to be.

> ✂ *LINKS*
> **Read more about following your values in Chapter 4 (Doing the Right Thing).**

One way to start figuring out the values that are important to you is to think about your heroes or the people you admire. You might admire a historical figure, a sports star, a friend, a teacher, or a relative. You could even admire a character in a book or movie.

Whoever your hero is, you can learn about your values by thinking about what you admire in that person. Whether you know it or not, usually the reason you admire someone has something to do with the values that person represents.

For example, one person I admire is Eleanor Roosevelt. (You'll see a quote from her later in this book!) Some people know her only as the wife of President Franklin Delano Roosevelt, but she was also an incredibly smart and accomplished person herself. Before she ever became First Lady, she was a writer; a supporter of women's rights; an activist who worked for racial equality, better living conditions for poor people, and world peace; an important political figure; and the founder of a school for girls where she taught for years. And she did all that in the early 1900s, when women weren't supposed to do *any* of those things. I admire all the things Eleanor Roosevelt did, but I also admire her strength, and the way she did exactly what she wanted to do and what she thought was important and right, no matter what other people said. Those values are just as important to me as all of the great things she worked for.

⬤▶*WRITE IT!* Name someone whom you admire.

_____

Why do you admire this person? List a few reasons.

_____

_____

_____

What positive values does this person represent to you? For example, if you said you admire your parents because they work hard to support the family, then maybe hard work and taking care of family are important values they represent to you. If you admire Harry Potter because he's so brave, then maybe being brave even when you feel scared is something you value.

✳*WORK IT!* Get together with a few of your friends to make a _hero tree_. First, find a medium-sized tree branch that has lots of little branches coming off it (look around on the

33

ground in your backyard or a park). Get an adult to help you stick the base of the branch into a thick piece of foam, cardboard, or wood so it stands up like a tree. Next, cut out lots of leaf shapes from construction paper, in different colors. You can trace a real leaf or make up your own shape — just make sure each leaf is really big, like around the size of this page. Each person should take a bunch of leaves. On one side of each leaf, write the name of someone you admire (like "my mom," "Michael Jordan," "Abraham Lincoln," "Amelia Earhart"). On the other side, write down the things you admire about that person — the values they represent to you. Trade leaves, and check out who your friends admire and why. If you want, decorate the leaves with paint, stickers, glitter, or your own designs. Tape or glue the leaves to the branch, so it looks like a real tree.

WRITE IT! On a separate piece of paper, list 10 values that are important to you. (Some examples: being open-minded, respecting your parents, being a caring friend, never lying, taking care of the environment, caring about animals.) For each one, try to think of something you did in the past month that is an example of following that value. So, if you list "not talking about people behind their backs" as one of your values, an example could be, "I walked away when everyone was gossiping about the new kid." (If you can't think of an example, create an example of how you would act in a made-up situation.)

✹*WORK IT!* One way to keep your values at the center of your life is to find a way to remind yourself of them. You can do this by making a *promise page*. (I call it that because, in a sense, values are like promises you make to yourself.) Take a sheet of paper or poster board and, using markers, paints, or pens, list the values that are important to you. You can write them out in a list like in the last exercise, or write them out in a few sentences (perhaps starting with "I believe . . ." or "I promise to always . . ."). Decorate your promise page however you like: Draw or paint a border, illustrate each value with drawings or pictures cut out of magazines, write each value in a different color and in a funky shape (like making the words spiral around in a circle), cover the page with glitter, sequins, dried leaves, or bottle caps — anything that looks cool to you! You can make it small enough to paste inside a journal or big enough to hang in your room, where you'll see it all the time. If you want, leave some extra space so you can keep adding to it as you discover other values that matter to you.

Valuing your goals

Values aren't the only things that determine how you live your life. Your goals and dreams are just as important in shaping how you act and what's important to you. As you figure out different goals that you might want to achieve, you'll learn about what kinds of accomplishments are valuable and

%*LINKS*
You'll find more on setting goals and making your dreams come true in *Creativity*, Chapter 7 (Dreaming and Doing).

important to you. Those goals can help you decide what you think are the most important ways to spend your time.

➤ *WRITE IT!* What are some goals you'd like to achieve? List a few, big or small. (Some examples: making new friends, getting an A in a class, learning a new piece on the piano, being a track star by the time you get to high school, becoming a chess grand master, finishing a really hard book.)

_____

_____

_____

_____

_____

_____

Pick one of these goals. What is an important thing you need to do to reach that goal (like study more, make an effort to talk to people, practice piano, set aside time to read)?

_____

37

In the last exercise, you just used your goals to set priorities for yourself. **Priorities** are the things that you decide are most important to you, like practicing the piano every day, studying, or spending time with your friends. When you have to choose between something that is a priority and something that isn't, the priority always wins.

Your priorities often come from your personal goals and dreams. If you've always wanted to be a chess champion, then one of your priorities might be to practice playing chess as much as you can. As you discover new goals, your priorities will change to fit those goals.

Priorities can also come from your values. For example, if being close to your family is one of your values and spending time with your little brother is an example of how you follow that value, then you might decide that hanging out with your brother every Saturday morning is a priority for you.

✓ ***REALITY CHECK*** Kate says, "My list of priorities is and always has been: 1. Schoolwork. 2. Family. 3. Social Life. That's because doing well in school and getting into a good college is important to me and my family."

Setting priorities

Priorities are important to discovering the whole you because **setting your priorities helps you to understand yourself better.** In order for something to be a priority, you have to think about how it fits into your whole life and the way you see yourself. So if you see yourself as an artist, then making time to paint or draw might be a priority for you. If you want to be healthier, then exercising and eating nutritious meals might be a priority for you.

Right now, your parents might set a lot of your priorities for you — like, "No e-mail until your homework is done!" You can't avoid the priorities that your parents set for you — not without getting in a lot of trouble, anyway! But you can make the things you have to do a little easier to deal with. Try these ideas:

- **Combine your priorities with theirs.** Say your parents think schoolwork should be your number-one priority, but you'd rather put friends first.

You can put the two together by arranging a weekly study date with a friend from class. Set up in the living room, at the kitchen table, or some other place where your parents can see that you're really studying, then quiz each other on vocabulary words or tackle some math problems together. (Be sure to schedule in study breaks!)

- **Reward yourself.** Set up a rewards system so you'll feel more motivated to tackle your parents' priorities. You could negotiate a deal with your mom that for every A you bring home on a big paper or test, you'll earn five minutes of phone time with your friends. Or reward yourself — for every twenty minutes of studying or piano practice completed, treat yourself to a piece of your favorite candy or three minutes with your soccer ball.

The older you get, the more you'll get to make your own choices about personal priorities. That's when exploring who you are and what you want becomes even more important. Maybe you'll choose priorities that are different from what your parents would choose —

like, say they want you to be a musician, but you decide that you want to spend time trying different sports instead or vice versa. There are millions of possibilities out there that you can choose to add to your life.

I had to make a big decision about my priorities when I was in high school. I started playing violin when I was just four, so by the time I was a teenager I was pretty good. But when I started high school, I joined tons of activities — swim team, Key Club, French Club, and debate, just to name a few — and I was so busy that I practiced the violin less and less. During one of my violin lessons, my teacher could tell that I hadn't practiced at all. She stopped the lesson and told me that I had to think seriously about how important playing the violin really was to me. If I decided that continuing to get better at my instrument wasn't a priority, we could make my lessons less intense — but if I wanted to keep being serious about playing the violin, I would have to make practicing a priority, or else we were both wasting our time.

I was pretty upset that she gave me an ultimatum like that, but I spent the whole week thinking about it. Eventually, I decided that playing the violin was such an important part of who I was and who I wanted to be — maybe even the *most* important part — that I wanted to make practicing one of my very top priorities. Little by little, I cut out most of my less-important activities, so I would have more time for the things that were most important to me.

✓ ***REALITY CHECK*** For Chelsye, figuring herself out and spending time with friends have always been big priorities. But as time goes by and grades and activities become more important, she's had to make adjustments to her priorities. "My biggest decision was when I was asked to be the assistant editor of the school paper," she says. "I was so pressed for time already, and this would drain another ten hours a week out of me."

Chelsye weighed all her other priorities, including school, friends, Key Club, and 4-H. Since she wants to be involved in writing or journalism when she's older, she decided to reorganize her priorities to be able to go for this opportunity. "I had to consider what was more important to me and what was most urgent," she says. "Homework was obviously urgent and important. I just organized my 4-H meetings for every other week and worked around Key Club so I wouldn't overexert myself. If I can't do something, I just say that I'm unavailable."

Evaluating priorities helped Chelsye and me make big decisions, but priorities also help you make small, everyday decisions. If you want to get good grades, then being a better student will be a priority for you, and you'll choose doing your homework over watching TV. If you know that spending time with your family is a bigger priority than spending time with your friends, then you'll pick going to your grandma's birthday party over spending Saturday at the mall.

One last thing: Setting priorities isn't just about cutting things *out* of your life. Remember, part of the point of **The Whole You** is exploration, which means trying lots of new things. Maybe one of your priorities could be to try tons of different things and not limit yourself to just one!

"WRITE IT!" List 10 things that you'd like to make a priority for yourself right now. (Some examples: being there for your best friend when she has a problem, learning how to skateboard, hanging out with your sister, spending time with your parents, reading one new book a month, saving money to buy a CD player, getting an A on your next math test.) For each one, name one thing you've done in the last month that illustrates how it's already a priority, *or* name something that you *could* do in the next month. So if saving money is a priority, you might give the example, "I decided not to buy those cool new jeans I wanted," or promise yourself, "I'm going to save half of my allowance every week this month." When you're done writing them all out, put a star next to the one you think should be *most* important.

Priority #1: _____

Example: _____

Priority #2: _____

Example: _____

Priority #3: _____

Example: _____

Priority #4: _____

Example: _____

Priority #5: _____

Example: _____

Priority #6: _____

Example: _____

Priority #7: _____

Example: _____

Priority #8: _____

Example: _____

Priority #9: _____

Example: _____

Priority #10: _____

Example: _____

Of course, we don't spend every waking minute on our priorities. Every day is filled with things that are priorities and things that are not. Some things, like going to a movie or hanging out with friends, are just fun ways to spend time. (Ideally, some of your priorities are fun for you,

✂ *LINKS*
Hop over to Chapter 4 (Doing the Right Thing) for more on making choices that fit in with your priorities.

45

Did you know?
If you spend five minutes a day brushing your teeth (figure an average of two and a half minutes morning and night), you'll spend 1,825 minutes a year, or more than 30 hours, on dental hygiene. That doesn't include flossing, picking stuff out of your braces, or getting those fluoride treatments.

too!) Other things are important daily tasks, maybe even essential, but not something you'd call a priority. (For example, you probably get dressed every day without fail, but I'll bet you didn't list "Get dressed every day" as one of your priorities!)

In a perfect world, you'd have plenty of time for all your priorities, all the important day-to-day stuff, *and* all the fun you wanted. In real life, the day-to-day stuff (gym class, riding the bus home, flossing) tends to take up tons of time. Sometimes you need to make an extra effort to make sure you take care of your priorities — and have fun, too.

"WRITE IT!" On a separate piece of paper, write down everything you've done in the past two days, besides eating and sleeping. Your list could include things like: went to school, did homework, e-mailed some friends, watched

TV, read a magazine, set the table for dinner, took out the trash, played with the dog, made my bed, tried to find a book I lost, brushed my teeth, took a shower, went grocery shopping with my mom.

Now, mark each thing on your list that's a priority with a P, and everything that's just fun with an F. (If something is neither, just leave it blank.) Do you have some Ps and some Fs every day? How can you fit in more time for your priorities?

✳ *WORK IT!* On a long roll of paper (or a bunch of smaller sheets taped together), draw your *ideal* day. You could draw yourself moving through the day (like a comic strip), or snapshots from different pieces of the day, or a series of images that represent the things you did that day (like a cereal bowl to represent breakfast, a school bus to show how you got to school, or a soccer ball to represent practice or a big game). What kinds of things are important for you to include?

✷*WORK IT!* This week, try to do something that's a priority every day. (Use your list of priorities to remind yourself of things you can do.) To help you do this, every night, write down what you did that day (like in the **◗*WRITE IT!*** above). Try to fit in some fun playtime every day, too.

✷*WORK IT!* Having trouble motivating yourself to squeeze in your priorities (or your parents' priorities)? To help make a priority more appealing, try to find at least one aspect of it that you *do* enjoy and focus on that to make your "chore" more fun. Love music in general but hate practicing your cello? Set aside five minutes of your daily practice time to play along with your favorite pop tunes. Love your family but think family game night is too dorky for words? Organize a family hike, a scavenger hunt, a cooking fest, or some other activity that you *would* enjoy.

✂*LINKS*
Check out *Friends and Family,* Chapter 1 (Family), for some fun activities to try with your parents.

Figuring out what matters

How do we learn our values and priorities? Lots of times, our values come from our parents, our religious communities, or the people around us, like our teachers, neighbors, coaches, or friends. Our communities and especially our parents play a major role in shaping our most fundamental values — like the ones that say it's wrong to kill or steal from other people, or the most basic beliefs that your religion or culture instills in you from birth.

✔ ***REALITY CHECK*** Christina's parents taught her to value their religious beliefs. Sydney's friends taught her the importance of sticking up for herself. Shauna learned from her parents to treat others the way she wants to be treated. Kate's father established that valuing education was important in their family.

But as you grow older, you might find yourself taking a closer look at the values of your church, family, or friends. You will decide for yourself the values you hold, the same way you'll start to set your own priorities. Being able to think critically about the values that other people encourage you to have, and deciding for yourself whether those values work for you is an important part of getting to know yourself as a whole, independent person.

✓ *REALITY CHECK* Izzy knows the importance of questioning the values other people present to you. She says, "If you don't speak up for yourself when you disagree with other people's values, and you just agree with them, then you start to pick up values that aren't good."

When you take a look at the values that surround you, you might decide that most of them work pretty well for you. On the other hand, you might find that a value held by your parents or your religion doesn't feel right to you anymore. Or you might decide to adopt a new value that isn't important to your friends. Your values and priorities can change over time, so sometimes you might change your mind about a value you've held in the past.

✓ ***REALITY CHECK*** Courtney was brought up with certain religious beliefs. "My parents always told me about heaven and how there's an afterlife," she says. "As I've gotten older, I still believe in God, but I don't believe in heaven anymore. There are other parts of the religion that I don't believe, either." For her, it's about making her *own* decisions about her beliefs: "It's important to me to believe what I think is right, instead of believing something just because other people tell me to."

Amy has developed some very important values on her own. "My parents have never taught me to be tolerant of other people; it's something I have learned myself," she says. Though she still holds on to other values her parents taught her, she's decided that in certain things, she wants to choose her own way. "By talking to my friends, I've found that many of our parents are almost bigots. They grew up in a different time period when racial and ethnic terms were used really without any consequence. Things are different with kids of our generation."

Sticking to your values

It's not always easy to stick to your values one hundred percent of the time. That's especially true when you're trying to decide whether to make a value your own.

> "Parents can only give good advice or put them on the right paths, but the final forming of a person's character lies in their own hands."
> — Anne Frank, diarist

You're trying it on, so you're not sure how to make it work for you. You might slip up once in a while — that's okay. (Maybe you've resolved not to gossip, but you can't resist passing on a juicy piece of dirt about someone you don't like; or maybe you think protecting the environment is really important, but you get lazy one day and dump a soda can behind a bush.) It doesn't mean that you have to ditch that value — it just means that you have to work a little harder to stick to it.

On the other hand, some values you explore *won't* feel worth sticking to. Sometimes, you might try on a new value but find it doesn't work for you. Maybe you'll come back to some older values, or maybe you'll move on to other new ones. Everyone goes through this — it's just a natural part of figuring out which values fit into your life.

☀ *WORK IT!* Sit down with a parent, an older relative, a teacher, a religious leader, or another adult you respect. (You can pick more than one!) Ask these adults questions about their current and past values — brainstorm a list beforehand. Some questions you could include:

- What values are important to you?
- When did you develop these values, and how? Why are they important to you?
- Are there any values that you tried out when you were younger but decided weren't for you? What made you change your mind about them?
- Are there things about your values that you've learned from experience that you wish you'd known sooner?

Are any of their answers surprising?

One thing that sometimes makes it hard to follow your values is when you feel like you're the only person who has those values. As you start to figure out more of your values and priorities on your own, you might find that sometimes they conflict with the values or priorities of people around you, whether they're those closest to you or total strangers. (I used to get into tons of arguments with my ninth grade English teacher, whose political values were the complete opposite of mine!)

But even when you disagree with someone's values, it's important to show respect for their beliefs. Exploring and setting your own values doesn't mean trashing the things that other people believe in. Listening to someone else's point of view can teach you about the kind of person they are and can even help you understand your own values better.

Growing up in Wisconsin, I was surrounded by kids who went hunting with their dads every fall. The first day of deer hunting season, it seemed like half the guys in school were absent. Hunting was a way of life there — but the problem was, I thought hunting was wrong. I used to get into arguments with guys in my classes all the time. It probably would have been a lot easier to just keep quiet, but I was really passionate about it, and I thought it was important to voice my views.

The interesting thing was that, as I argued with these guys, I actually learned a lot about why people like to hunt, and I started to understand it better. Even though I still didn't agree with them, taking the time to listen to what they said showed me that they were really committed to their point of view, too. And I also learned a lot about my own values — for example, the guys pointed out that I was arguing against hurting animals but I still ate meat, which really made me think about why I believed the things I did and how they fit together.

> **&**✂️**LINKS***
> **Flip to Chapter 5 (Accepting Yourself — and Everyone Else) for more on understanding and accepting the values and beliefs of others.**

Things get trickier when your values bring you in conflict with people who are closer to you, like family and friends.

✔ ***REALITY CHECK*** Courtney gets into a lot of fights with her uncle, whose views on race and religion are radically different from hers. "He has a one-sided view of everything," she says. "I found I can't be around him without him discouraging my values. I tell him what I think, but he is set in his ways and won't listen to a fifteen-year-old." After trying unsuccessfully to have a reasonable conversation with her uncle, Courtney settled on a final solution to avoid fighting all the time: "I avoid the topics of religion, politics, and world events."

You don't have to try to change everyone else's mind — with people like Courtney's uncle, that's pretty much impossible, anyway. But you do need to know how to hold firmly to your own values — maybe even stand up for them once in a while.

Sticking by what you believe in, even when people around you don't agree, is the ultimate test of your values. That's because to defend your beliefs or stand by them in the face of challenges, you need to have a firm grip on why you believe what you do. Sometimes defending your beliefs can actually help you strengthen them.

When you have to stick up for yourself, it's helpful to keep a few things in mind:

- **Focus on why your beliefs are important to you.** Why do you believe what you believe? What makes this value right for you? The more confident you are in what you believe, the easier it will be to stand firm.

- **Plan your defense.** If you know that someone is going to attack your values, plan ahead and try to think of ways to defend yourself. Suppose you've decided that you don't want to join your friends in picking on a less popular kid anymore. Since you know your friends might question you or even make fun of you for it, come up with some things you can say in response. Depending on how you feel, you could try to convince them with an argument about why you think it's wrong, or you could just think of quick comebacks like, "Listen, I have better things to do."

- **Be respectful.** To defend your values, you don't have to trash someone else. People are more likely to listen to you and respect *your* values if you respect *them*. Take the example of your friends picking on another kid — even if you really believe that they're wrong, saying something like "I just don't think this is very fun" might be a lot more effective than "Why are you guys always such jerks?!"

- **Do what you believe.** Sticking up for your beliefs doesn't mean simply arguing about them. It also means acting on them. You might not be able to convince everyone else to stop picking on that kid, or to raise money for the homeless, or to recycle, but if *you* act according to your beliefs, at least you'll know you're doing what you think is right.

- **Realize that you're doing something really brave by standing up for yourself.** Stay strong!

"Trust yourself. Think for yourself. Act for yourself. Speak for yourself. Be yourself."
— Marva Collins, educator

✔ ***REALITY CHECK*** "My town is very conservative, and I'm not," says Maeve. "I meet people every day who have different beliefs than me. It's sad, but at times I feel like an outsider to my whole community. But in the end, it's made my beliefs even stronger."

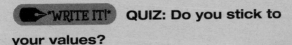

☀ *WORK IT!* Create a superhero who defends one of the values that's important to you. What will you name her (or him, or it)? What kind of costume should she wear? What will her special powers be? What are her weaknesses? What kind of "weapon" will she use to defend the value for which she fights? (Remember, a weapon doesn't have to be something that inflicts violence, especially if violence goes against your values. Wonder Woman fights her enemies with a special lasso that forces those she catches in it to tell the truth!) Draw your superhero in a comic strip, or design the movie poster.

✎ *WRITE IT!* QUIZ: Do you stick to your values?

Are you able to stand by what you believe in under pressure? Take this quiz and find out.

1. In class one day, your teacher starts railing about how your favorite TV show is immoral. Do you argue with him?

    a. No way!

    b. A little — you raise your hand and bring up some good points, but if he shows no sign of listening to your point of view, you eventually lay off.

    c. Heck, yeah — in fact, the two of you spend the rest of class duking it out.

2. You're hanging out with some people from school and one of them cracks a rude joke about a kid in your class. Everyone else laughs, but you think it's kind of mean. What do you do?

    a. Kind of half-laugh like you think it's funny, too — it would be too awkward to say anything.

    b. Say, "Come on, you guys, cut it out. That's not funny."

    c. Call the person who made the joke a !#@$* and storm off without waiting to hear the reaction.

3. You and your friend have completely different views on all kinds of moral and political issues. How do you deal with that?

a. You never really bring up your point of view — in fact, your friend doesn't even know your point of view on a lot of things.

b. You argue about stuff sometimes, but mostly you agree to disagree.

c. You would never have a friend who had such different views from you.

4. Your parents won't let you listen to certain bands or singers because they think they're bad role models. You think they're overreacting. What do you do?

a. Do what they say — how can you argue with your *parents*?

b. Try to explain to them that you understand how they feel, but you're definitely not going to go out and do any of the things that those people sing about.

c. Get in a huge fight with them about it and defiantly blast their most hated band at top volume.

5. Your friends find out you sometimes sleep with your old teddy bear. They totally make fun of you for it. Your reaction:

a. Dump Teddy in the trash. It's not worth being humiliated over.

b. Laugh with them, but keep giving Teddy the place of honor when you feel like it. So what if you need a little cuddle once in a while?

c. Dump your friends. If they don't understand you, they're losers.

5–7 points: You tend to cave too quickly when stuff you believe in is on the line. Maybe it's because you don't want to cause a fuss or because you don't think your feelings are worth sticking up for. Whatever it is, remember it's okay — heck, it's *important* — to take a stand once in a while. Start small — call someone out about an offensive joke. You'll feel a lot better when you know you tried to stick up for what you think is right.

SCORING: Give yourself one point for every "a" answer, two points for every "b," and three points for every "c."

8–11 points: Most of the time, you strike a good balance between voicing your views and being tactful. You're able to stand up for what's important to you without ticking off other people in the process. Just be careful that your skill for smoothing things over doesn't cause you to back down when it's really important, simply because you don't want a big confrontation.

> ✂ ***LINKS***
> **Read more about coping with conflict in *Friends and Family*, Chapter 5 (Connections and Conflict).**

12–15 points: No one could ever accuse you of being a pushover — you're always willing to stand up for your values. That's great — keep it up! But make sure that you give other people a chance to air *their* points of view, too — and give them the respect they deserve. And don't be afraid to make room in your life for friends who don't have the exact same views as you — you might just learn something from them.

Sometimes standing up for your values can be downright scary. Once, I was taking a speech class with a whole bunch of older kids. A couple of the older guys did a skit for the class that I thought was incredibly racist. (It happened to make fun of Asians, so I felt personally hurt as well.) I didn't say anything about it at the time — these guys practically ruled the school, so I was afraid to speak up. Besides, the whole class was laughing at the skit, and I thought they would all think I was a freak for making a fuss about it.

But a week or two later, we had to give a speech about something that made us angry. I chose to talk about the racist skit. I was so nervous I could actually feel my legs shaking as I began my speech, but as I got into it, I felt stronger and stronger, until I was pounding on the podium to emphasize my points. At first I couldn't bring my-self to look at the guys who did the skit, sitting together at the back of the classroom, but when I sat down, I glanced back and saw that they all had stunned, ashamed looks on their faces. I realized that they weren't scary or intimidating after all, and they weren't bad people. They had just never had anyone stand up and tell them that their racist remarks were wrong and hurt-ful. I felt proud that I had done something to teach them, but most of all, I was proud of myself for standing up for what was important to me.

LINKS
Read Chapter 4
(Doing the Right
Thing) for more
on making
tough choices.

"WRITE IT!" Try to remember the last time you disagreed with someone's action because that action went against your values. Did you say anything at the time? Imagine if you and that person were each asked to defend your position in a formal debate. What would you say to make your case? What would your "opponent" say? Write out the script!

It's not easy to stand up for your beliefs, but as long as you're open-minded, it's totally worth the challenge. You'll strengthen your beliefs, stand up for what's right, and probably learn a lot about someone else's beliefs, too. You'll also discover how strong you can be!

Chapter Three
The Way You Feel

Getting to know your emotions

The anger bubbles up inside you before you know it, and you run to your room and slam the door. Frustrated, you punch your pillow and fight back the tears pricking at the corners of your eyes. How can this be happening to you?

Sound familiar? These days, you're probably experiencing lots of different feelings. And because of the way your body works as you get older, your feelings will get stronger and more unpredictable, too. That goes for ones that feel good, like feeling happy or silly, and ones that feel bad, like being mad or sad.

Your emotions form a major part of the core of your spirit. They're what drive you to act a certain way or choose a set of values. Your feelings help you decide who your friends are or what you want to be when you grow up. They can help you decide whether you like the way your life is (if you're happy or excited) and motivate you to change things in your life to make it better (if you're sad, angry, or frustrated). So understanding the way you feel inside is an important part of exploring the whole you.

> "Cherish your own emotions and never undervalue them."
> — Robert Henri, painter

Getting to know all your different emotions — even the yucky ones — and learning how to deal with them strengthens your spirit and gives you a more solid core. The first step is to be able to recognize the different feelings you have. Here are just some of the emotions that we all feel from time to time:

JOY is, hands-down, my favorite emotion of all. Joy is intense pleasure and happiness, that feeling you get when you want to sing and dance and hug everyone in sight, when you feel all sorts of wonderful things bubbling around in your chest and

> "Find ecstasy in life; the mere sense of living is joy enough."
> — Emily Dickinson, poet

you think you're going to burst with delight. Joy can be quieter, too, like when you just feel so good you can't help smiling.

✔ ***REALITY CHECK*** Sydney was incredibly happy when she got her dog, Dexter, for her birthday. "My parents told me we were going to a farm to milk cows and stuff like that," she says. "But instead, I got to pick out a puppy!"

WRITE IT! Make a *joy book.* In a notebook or blank book, start listing everything you can think of that makes you smile or brings you joy. List things at random — you might include everything from "fun birthday parties" to "winning a race" to "my little cousin's laugh." Decorate the pages and cover if you want to — write in different colors, doodle designs on the pages, glitz it up with glitter, or add drawings and pictures to illustrate the things that make you happy. Keep adding to the book as you think of new things, and ask your friends and family to contribute things that make *them* happy, too. (You could give each friend a whole page to write on and decorate!) Peek into your joy book whenever you feel like smiling!

WORK IT! Send a happiness package to someone you love. Fill a box or big envelope with stuff you think will make them smile —

corny jokes, pictures of the two of you together, a tape or CD of happy songs, a sprinkling of confetti, the recipient's favorite candy, anything you can think of. Decorate the box or envelope with happy drawings, collages, words, designs. Mail it, or deliver it in person!

> **"Our goal should be to achieve joy."**
> — Ana Castillo, poet, essayist, and feminist

SADNESS is the opposite of joy. While joy makes you feel like you're flying up, up, up, sadness drags you down. (When we're sad, we often say we're "down in the dumps" or "feeling low.") Sometimes when you're sad you feel like crying or crawling into bed or hiding from everyone. You might say that you feel miserable, heartbroken, hurt, or just plain yucky.

✓ ***REALITY CHECK*** "Because of his job, my dad has to spend six months out of the year living in Canada," says Shauna. "It's great when he's here, but when he has to leave again it makes me so sad, because I miss him so much."

69

✒ "WRITE IT!" When was the last time you felt sad? What made you sad, and why?

_____

_____

_____

_____

Imagine that you're a famous advice columnist and someone has written to you with this exact same situation. What advice would you give? What would you tell them to help them feel better? Write out what you would say.

✷ "WORK IT!" Think of some things that make you feel better when you're sad, like talking to a friend, snuggling up in bed with your favorite book, getting a hug, taking a long shower, playing with your puppy. Write them down. Share your list with your mom or dad or a friend, and ask them what they do when _they_ feel sad. Does anyone else have something on their list that you haven't thought of? Can you try something from one of their lists to see if it works for you?

70

FEAR is that feeling you get when you're worried something bad might happen. When you're afraid, you feel nervous and anxious. You might feel butterflies in your stomach or get sweaty palms, you might feel tense all over or have a creepy feeling that you don't want to know what's going to happen next. Sometimes it's reasonable to be afraid, say, if you see a car zooming toward you or if there's a creepy guy hanging out by your school — after all, one of the reasons we feel fear is to help us recognize dangerous situations. Other times, fear can hold you back, like when you're scared to talk in class or tell someone how you really feel. No one is totally fearless — but everyone can learn to be brave and take action in spite of their fears.

> "The only thing we have to fear is fear itself."
> — Franklin Delano Roosevelt, thirty-second President of the United States

✔ ***REALITY CHECK*** After seeing the movie *Cast Away,* Christina is afraid to fly. Izzy gets scared and nervous when she has to confront a stranger: "Once I went to McDonald's and they gave me the wrong order. I was too scared to tell them that it was wrong, so I took

71

it anyway, even though it was more expensive than what I had ordered."

WRITE IT! What are you afraid of? List five things.

_____

_____

_____

_____

_____

WRITE IT! Now list five things you're *not* afraid of, but other people are.

_____

_____

_____

_____

_____

WORK IT! Design a haunted house in which you'd actually be afraid. What kinds of scary things would happen there? Draw your haunted house, write out a detailed description, or build a model of it.

HOPE is what lets us see the possibility of better times and brighter days ahead. When you hope, you're dreaming about or wishing for something that you'd like to come true, whether it's a trip to Disney World, a part in the school play, an end to racism, or a cure for a deadly disease.

> "We must accept finite disappointment, but never lose infinite hope."
> — Martin Luther King Jr., civil rights leader

Feeling hopeful helps you to look at life positively, even if things aren't going so well. If we couldn't look forward to our fondest hopes, we'd never have the dedication to work to make them happen.

✔ ***REALITY CHECK*** Chelsye hopes to publish a successful novel someday — she's already written a few books. By writing constantly, she's working on getting better and better so she can make her hope a reality.

☙ ***LINKS***
In a hopeful mood? Check out *Creativity*, Chapter 7 (Dreaming and Doing), to read about turning hopes and dreams into reality.

✎ ***WRITE IT!*** What is something you hope for? When you think about it, how do you feel inside?

_____

_____

★"WORK IT!" Think of one small step you can take to help make the thing you hope for happen. If you hope that there will be a cure for cancer someday, could you participate in a walkathon or other event that raises money for research (or organize one yourself)? If you hope to become an actor, could you audition for the school play? Now, go out and do it!

★"WORK IT!" Create a *hope box* for yourself or someone you care about. Put things in it that represent hope and good possibilities, like a drawing of someone you admire, some inspiring quotes, a poem you wrote about the first day of spring, or pictures of things that make you feel hopeful. Don't forget to decorate it!

ANGER burns from the inside out. When you're angry, you feel hostile and negative toward someone or something. You might want to kick or punch something, scream, or slam doors. Often, being really mad feels like there's something hot or burning inside you — if you get really worked up, your body might even feel warmer. That's why we sometimes compare anger to heat and fire — we say that someone is "boiling over" or "needs to blow off steam," or that a person is "burning up" with rage. You might get angry when someone hurts your feelings or does something annoying or mean to you. You can even get angry at yourself sometimes.

✓ **"REALITY CHECK"** Shauna was chatting online one day with some girls she knew. "I typed 'be right back' and stepped away from the computer for a minute, and when I got back, they left the chat room right away," she remembers. Shauna scrolled up to read what the other girls were talking about and found out they had been saying nasty things about her — boy, was she mad!

"WRITE IT!" What are some things that make you angry? List two or three. For each one, can you also think of why that thing makes you angry? One example: "When I find out that a friend talked about me behind my back, it makes me angry because it hurts my feelings

75

when I trust someone and that person betrays my trust."

☀*WORK IT!* Next time you feel mad, blow off steam by doing something physical, like running around your yard, boxing, dancing, or hitting tennis balls — anything that gets you moving. The key: Try doing it *before* you do anything else to react to feeling mad, like yelling at the person you're mad at, complaining to someone else, or getting even.

►*WRITE IT!* Think about the last time you got really, really mad at someone. Why were you angry? Did you tell them? How did it turn out? On a separate piece of paper, write about or draw what happened. If you weren't happy about how it turned out, write about or draw what you *wish* had happened.

PRIDE means feeling good about yourself or something you've done. When you feel proud, you stand taller and feel a confident, satisfied glow inside.

Sometimes you're proud about something that's recognized by other people, like when you win an award or perform well in a play. Other times, you might take pride in more personal things, like putting in hours of hard work studying or sticking to your beliefs.

✿*LINKS*
Read more about taking pride in all your parts in Chapter 5 (Accepting Yourself — and Everyone Else).

✔ ***REALITY CHECK*** "I'm proud of my heritage," says Christina. "I'm one hundred percent Italian." Sydney's proud of the hard work she puts into gymnastics practice.

▶***WRITE IT!*** What are five things that you're proud of?

1. _____

2. _____

3. _____

4. _____

5. _____

WORK IT! Make a list of five things that you're proud of about a friend, and have your friend do the same for you. Trade lists to give each other a boost!

EMBARRASSMENT is feeling self-conscious or ashamed about something. You might feel embarrassed if someone makes fun of you, if you're in an uncomfortable situation, or if you're shy. You also can feel embarrassed in good situations, like when someone says tons of wonderful things about you in front of other people. When you're embarrassed, you might blush or feel nervous sensations like your heart pounding.

REALITY CHECK Sydney had a totally embarrassing moment when she was in her school's production of *Annie*. "It's hard enough just being onstage with everyone looking at you," she says. "But during one performance, I was daydreaming and forgot to say my lines!"

☞ "WRITE IT!" What's your most embarrassing moment ever?

_____

_____

_____

_____

✳ "WORK IT!" Ask your parents, grandparents, or other adults about their most embarrassing moments when they were your age. How did they feel about what happened then? How do they feel about it now?

LOVE is caring deeply about someone. You feel affectionate toward the people you love, you care about their safety, and you want them to be happy. You probably want to do nice things for them, too. There are all different kinds of love; you can love your parents, your friends, your pet, a boyfriend or girlfriend, all in different ways.

> "Love cures people, the ones who receive love and the ones who give it, too."
> — Karl A. Menninger, psychiatrist

◀▷*WRITE IT!* Who do you love? Pick one person and make a list of five things you can do to show them how much you love them. (Some ideas: Write them a card telling them how important they are to you. Make them a birthday cake. Give them a foot rub. Hug them. Write them a poem. Treat them to a movie. Make a date to hang out, just the two of you. Buy their favorite candy.) Then do one!

1. _____

2. _____

3. _____

4. _____

5. _____

⚙*LINKS*
To read about how your relationships with the people you love can make you more whole, go to *Friends and Family.*

※*WORK IT!* Don't limit yourself to just one person! This week, try to do something nice every day for someone you love. (It'll make you feel good, too!)

Other emotions

WRITE IT! What are some other emotions besides the eight described here? On a separate piece of paper, name a few, and for each one, think of five words that go with that emotion.

We've been talking about each emotion separately, but the truth is that you rarely feel one emotion all by itself. Different emotions overlap and work with and against one another. You can feel several emotions at the same time — sadness and anger, for example, or joy and hope, or even fear and joy. And it's even easy to mistake one emotion for another as they mingle together inside you.

WORK IT! "Act out" each of the emotions mentioned in this chapter. What kinds of movements go with each one — fluid, jumpy, quick, slow, spastic? How are the movements you make to express each emotion similar — for example, could you jump up and down for both joy and anger? How are the movements different? Does moving in a happy way make you feel happier? Take turns acting out the emotions with a friend, and see if you can guess which emotion the other one is doing.

☀"WORK IT!" Go through magazines and newspapers and cut out pictures of people with different types of facial expressions. In each picture, what kind of emotion(s) is the person feeling? How can you tell? Do any of the emotions look similar? See if you can imitate the different expressions. How does it feel?

Did you know?
Smiling can actually lift your mood when you're feeling down. There's something about the physical act of smiling that activates happier parts of your brain. (That's the highly unscientific explanation, anyway!)

Dealing with it

It's fun to feel joy, hope, or love. But when what you're feeling doesn't feel so great — like when you're sad, angry, or afraid — it's harder to know how to deal.

There's no such thing as an emotion that's wrong or bad. You've got a right to any feelings you have. In fact, unpleasant emotions can actually be good for you sometimes, because they signal when something's wrong in your life (like a friend who always hurts your feelings) and motivate you to make a change (like getting rid of that hurtful friend).

But there *are* good and bad ways of dealing with difficult emotions. **Bad ways of dealing are *destructive* to the whole you** — they don't help you solve your problems, they're bad for your health, or they make you feel even worse. Some destructive ways of dealing are:

- Taking your anger or frustration out on someone else — especially if that person's not the one you're mad at. (That's like when you snap at your mom just because you had a bad day at school.) All that does is hurt someone else's feelings.
- "Getting even." Sure, taking revenge on someone might look like a lot of fun on TV or in a movie. But it doesn't really solve anything. You're not making yourself feel better, you're just spreading the bad feelings around.
- Wallowing in your yucky feelings. You're *totally* entitled to feel bad, no matter what anyone says. (I hate it when people chirp, "Cheer up!" when

you're feeling lousy, don't you?) But if all you can do is think about how miserable you are, it's really hard to do anything to fix the situation or make yourself feel better. That's wallowing, and it doesn't help you. If anything, it makes you feel worse.

- Checking out of life. When you withdraw from everyone around you, you're cutting yourself off from people who might be able to help and support you. You're also more likely to wallow in your painful feelings and get stuck there.

- Squashing your feelings down and pretending they're not there.

If you do that, it's like cleaning your room by shoving everything into the closet and closing the door. Sure, you don't have to look at the mess, but now you can't use your closet! **Denying what you feel closes off a part of the whole you.** And you *definitely* don't want to do that. The other problem with squashing down feelings is that, sooner or later, they're bound to explode, mak-

> ❧***LINKS***
> **When you feel like withdrawing, that's often when it's most important to connect with others. See** *Friends and Family,* **Chapter 6 (Coping), for more on getting help from other people.**

ing you feel even worse than if you had dealt with them to begin with. (Think of shoving your messes and clutter into your closet day after day, until the closet is so full and overflowing that the door bursts open!)

- Using drugs and alcohol. I'm sure you've heard plenty about how bad *that* is for you. It's bad for your health, and you've got too much going for you to waste time with that stuff. Plus, drugs and alcohol are just another way of pretending your feelings aren't there, which we know is bad.

✓ ***REALITY CHECK*** Cricket used to try to squash all those bad feelings down without dealing with them. It didn't work very well. "I was an emotional powder keg ready to explode. Anything and anyone would set me off. It feels like you're in a Tilt-A-Whirl that's not stopping and never will."

Good ways of dealing are *constructive* — they help you vent your feelings and move past them, they help you find a way to fix whatever's making you feel bad, or they just plain boost your mood. They can help you explore the whole you, too, as you learn about what sets you off and what you need to feel good.

✓ ***REALITY CHECK*** Everyone has their own favorite way to cope when they're mad or sad. Shauna says, "I call a friend or write in my diary." Sydney likes to play with her dog. Christina says, "I go in my room, put on loud music, and dance around!"

These days, Cricket has found better ways to deal. "Now, whenever I'm in a bad mood, I turn on my radio and listen to music. I also try to find a way to work it out of my system — running or writing a poem about it both work when I'm angry."

Some constructive ways of dealing are:

- Talking about what's bothering you — calling a friend, like Shauna does, or venting to your mom or dad or someone else you trust. Not only can it help you come up with a solution for your problems, talking through what happened can help you figure out *why* it happened and how to keep the problem from happening again.

- Letting yourself have a good cry. Sometimes you just need to feel sad. A cryfest also lets you get a lot of the sadness out of your system, so you can start to feel better. (Just be careful not to get stuck in crying mode — more than a day or two and you're not getting anywhere.)

> **Did you know?**
> Crying can be good for you. When you're upset, the tears you produce are full of stress chemicals — crying is nature's way of getting them out of your system.

- Working out your frustrations. Getting your blood pumping can boost your mood and help work out any twitchy irritation. Dancing in your room (like Christina) is really good for this, but so is going for a run (like Cricket) or a long walk, beating up your pillow, or any other physical activity. Doing something physical also blows off steam and can help keep you from boiling over with anger or frustration, which makes it a lot easier to think clearly about what's bothering you.

> **✄ *LINKS***
> Flip to *Body and Mind,* **Chapter 3 (Working It),** for more ways to get your blood pumping.

- Hanging out with folks who love and support you. That could mean going to a friend's house, bonding with your parents, playing with your pet (like Sydney does) — as long as you're with someone who reminds you how loved you are.

- Writing it out. Keeping a journal lets you spill onto the page whatever's stressing you out instead of keeping it locked up inside. It also helps you solve problems, deal with difficult emotions, and work through whatever is bothering you.

> ✂️ *LINKS*
> Check out more on journals and writing and how they can help you learn about the whole you, *Creativity*, Chapter 3 (Write On).

✔️ *REALITY CHECK* Chelsye found that keeping a journal not only helped her feel better, it helped her explore who she was. "I named my journal Ryan, so I thought of it more as a friend than a book. I recorded everything that happened to me, good things and bad, and I would ask myself questions about how I felt and what I wanted. Answering these questions of who I was and where I wanted to be really helped me find myself."

- Distracting yourself. Sometimes bad feelings can get so
  overwhelming that they get
  stuck in your head and you
  can't stop thinking about
  them. Distracting yourself,
  whether by finding something
  positive in your life to focus on, forcing yourself
  to think about homework, or just flipping on
  a silly sitcom, can clear your head
  and get you unstuck from your negative feelings so you don't wallow
  in them. Then, when you've calmed
  down a little, you can go back to try
  to figure out how to fix whatever
  made you feel bad.

Did you know?
When you're in a good mood, your brain works more creatively, and with more flexibility and complexity than when you're in a bad mood.

❀*LINKS*
See *Body and Mind,* Chapter 6 (Feeling Healthy), for more on staying emotionally healthy. *Friends and Family,* Chapter 6 (Coping), explores getting support from others.

Exploring your intuition

Now let's look at another kind of feeling: your intuition. *Intuition* is another word for your gut feelings,
the instincts that come from deep inside you. Have
you ever met someone for the first time and instantly
felt comfortable around them? Have you ever felt

a creeping sense of danger? That's your intuition at work.

Intuition often comes from a deeper sense of what's good for you. If you're doing something that goes against your true self, your intuition will usually send you a signal — you'll feel uncomfortable. On the other hand, when you're following a path that's good for you, your intuition may let you know by giving you a sense of peace and rightness. Intuition should never be *totally* in charge, but it adds a little extra information to help you navigate through life.

Understanding your intuition is a skill that has to be learned and practiced, like playing a musical instrument. Learning to interpret the signals your intuition is sending can be tricky — most of us aren't naturally good at telling the difference between true intuition and a passing impulse. But the more you explore your intuition's signals and the more you get to know who you are and who you want to be, the better you'll get at understanding what your gut is telling you.

✔ **"REALITY CHECK"** Jeff found that following his gut was a good move when he first got to middle school. "There were a lot of kids there who I didn't know because they went to different elementary schools," he explains. "Some people I just told myself to say hi to, and now we're friends. Others I decided not to talk to, and that worked out because those kids ended up being the troublemakers. Usually, I don't listen to my gut instinct, but in these cases it was right. I'm glad that I decided to say hi."

> "Self-trust is the first secret of success."
> — Ralph Waldo Emerson, philosopher, essayist, and poet

Amy wishes she had listened to her gut when she met a guy who was no good. "I knew from the beginning that he was bad news. On one level, I really wanted him to like me, and we went out for about two months. But on another level, I wanted to run. Every time I think back about it, I think, 'What was I doing?' I should have paid attention to my gut instinct."

Try these activities to tune in to your intuition:

✳ **"WORK IT!"** Try this the next time you're having trouble making up your mind about something: Find a quiet, peaceful place where you feel comfortable and safe — maybe your bedroom or backyard or a park. Get comfy — it doesn't matter whether you sit or lie down, whatever you prefer. Close your eyes and try to relax. When your body feels relaxed, concentrate on your decision. Imagine yourself deciding on one of your options — visualize it actually happening. How do you feel? How does your body feel? Do any words or images pop into your head? The thoughts and feelings that come up are what your intuition is trying to tell you. Pay attention to all these feelings, then imagine yourself deciding on the other option. Pay attention to what happens.

WORK IT! Some people swear their dreams help them make decisions or work out problems. To try it, pick a weekend night or other time when you won't have to wake up to an alarm clock. Put a pencil and paper next to your bed. Formulate your problem into a concrete question — writing it down can help you do this. When you go to bed, concentrate on your question, and try to hold it in your mind as you fall asleep. As soon as you wake up, grab your pencil and paper and write down everything you can remember about your dreams — and anything else that's floating in your head when you open your eyes. Write as quickly as you can without stopping. When you've gotten everything down, set it aside for a couple of hours, then read it over. The answer to your question probably won't be obvious — you may have to interpret the situation in your dreams.

✂ *LINKS*
For a fun take on the hidden meaning in your dreams, check out *Dream Journal* from Klutz, Inc.

Of course, you can't depend on your intuition to make all your decisions in life. If your brain isn't also participating, your gut can be kind of irresponsible sometimes. If I followed my gut feelings everywhere, I'd probably lie in bed all day, watch trashy TV, and eat lots of chocolate — and feel pretty sick after a few days!

We all get random urges that can mislead us. I remember once, when I was really little, I felt in my *soul* that I *had* to have this particular kind of candy. I felt I needed it so badly that if my mom wouldn't buy it for me, I should just take it from the store. That feeling certainly came from the depths of me, but it wasn't intuition — for one thing, stealing definitely goes against my values. Remember, real intuition should keep you whole. What I was feeling was an *impulse* — and when I stopped to think about it, I realized that it wasn't the right thing to do.

Maybe sometimes you feel the urge to cut school, do something dangerous, toss an eraser at a teacher, or spread nasty gossip. When you feel urges like that, it definitely comes from inside you, just like that thieving impulse I had when I was five. But acting on those impulses can often be bad for your spirit — and bad for you in other ways — like when you get in trouble!

So how do you tell the difference between an impulse and intuition? One easy way is to wait, say, a day. If the feeling or urge goes away, it was probably just an impulse. It's also very important to stop and *think* about what the feeling is telling you and whether it goes against common sense or reason. **Anything that urges you to go against your core values, do something you know is dangerous or destructive, or**

> "The more we know, the better our intuitions."
> — Christina Stead, novelist

94

abandon your highest priorities is not intuition — it's probably an impulse.

Your gut can also mislead you about people. It can sometimes be tricky to recognize the difference between having intuition about a person and making a snap judgment. A snap judgment is based on prejudice — it's making up your mind about someone based on superficial things, maybe what they're wearing or what they look like. Intuition, on the other hand, is based on unconscious signals and instincts.

When I first met Tess years ago, I didn't like her one bit. (Tess is not her real name; I've given her a fake name so her feelings won't be hurt!) I sized up her outfit, her neat, girly appearance, and the way she kind of kept to herself and immediately decided she was prissy and probably a snob. Tess and I eventually became great friends. It turns out she isn't prissy, she's just neat; and she isn't a snob, she's just kind of shy. If I had stuck to my initial snap judgment, I would have missed out on a really fun friend.

On the other hand, when I first met Dawn (also not her real name!), she seemed nice enough in the beginning. We hung out a lot, shopping and stuff like that, and we discovered that we had a lot in common. But I noticed after a while that I felt really uncomfortable and rushed every time we hung out. When I thought about it, I realized that Dawn always talked so much that she never listened to anything I said, and she was always cutting short our hang-out time to rush off to meet someone else. My uncomfortable instincts were right — not long after that, Dawn dumped me for some other friends that she thought were cooler.

Again, it's important to analyze what your feelings are telling you. If it's something like, "Well, he comes from Lincoln, of course he'll be a snob," then it probably has more to do with prejudice than intuition. But if it's something like "I don't like him — he's always sneering when he talks to me," or "I like her — there's something about her that seems so open," then that may be intuition at work. Try some of the previous exercises to help you figure out the difference.

Your intuition can be good at some things, like letting you know who your friends are, but terrible at others, like helping you plan for the future. And like

⚓ ***LINKS***
Turn to Chapter 4 (Doing the Right Thing) for more on using your intuition — and your brain — to help you make decisions.

anything else, it takes practice to learn how to figure out what your gut is telling you. So try not to let yourself be ruled by your gut feelings. Instead, think of your intuition as one more tool you can use to help you explore the whole you.

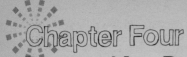

Chapter Four
Doing the Right Thing

Choices

Every day you're faced with choices. Some of them are simple, like what to wear in the morning or what to have for lunch. Others are a lot tougher, like deciding whether to do something when you see another kid getting picked on or figuring out how important it is to you to be popular in school. **Learning how to make choices that keep you whole is one of the biggest lessons of discovering the whole you.**

"It is our choices, Harry, that show what we truly are, far more than our abilities."
— Professor Dumbledore in *Harry Potter and the Chamber of Secrets*, by J.K. Rowling

Trying to figure out what choices work best for you can be confusing sometimes. Lots of factors come into play, including your values and priorities, your feelings and intuition, the influence of people around you, and more. So it's natural to struggle with your decisions sometimes. When it comes to tough decisions, even grown-ups have a hard time doing the right thing or even agreeing on what the right thing is. But the more you learn about making choices on your own and the more you do it, the better you'll get at it.

If you're naturally indecisive, even the littlest decisions can seem overwhelming or even impossible. I can't tell you how many hours of my life I've spent trying to figure out what to wear or what movie I want to see! For little decisions like that, I've found the best thing to do is just *choose*. If you must, set yourself a time limit (thirty seconds to decide what to order for dessert!) and play eeny-meeny-miney-moe, flip a coin, or close your eyes and point if you can't decide by the deadline. You'll probably wish you'd made a different decision sometimes, but there's no harm done, and at the very least you'll have learned something that you can use the next time you're faced with a similar decision.

But there are lots of choices you just can't make by closing your eyes and pointing. When you have a tough decision to make, you have to consider your values, feelings, and all the other factors I've mentioned. One way to figure out the right things to do is to take each possible option and ask yourself a few important questions:

The Choices Checklist

1. **How does this choice fit in with my values?** Is the option you're considering clearly aligned with or against one of your important values? Look at the list of values you made in Chapter 2 if you need to be reminded.

✓ **"REALITY CHECK"** Amy got sidetracked from her values because of a decision she made. "I was friends with a girl who was in the 'bad' crowd, and the decision I made was to be a member of the group," she explains. "It was the wrong decision. I started smoking and doing things I had to hide from my parents, and I regret that beyond belief. I got caught in EVERYTHING by my parents and was grounded for six months. But I don't blame them one bit. I grew up in a very moral house, and I was taught values and respect, but I defied them all in what I did."

2. **How does this choice fit in with my priorities?** Is this option something that is normally a priority

for you? Is this option something that isn't a priority but should be? Reread your list of priorities from Chapter 2. Will making this decision require you to rethink or adjust your priorities? Does choosing this option mean you have to sacrifice one of your priorities?

3. **How do I feel about my choice?** Does the thought of this option make you feel happy, sad, angry, embarrassed, proud, guilty? If you make a choice, will you be comfortable with the feelings that go with it?

4. **What does my gut tell me?** Try one of the intuition exercises in Chapter 3. Does your instinct tell you that this option is okay? Or try flipping a coin to decide. If you're disappointed by the result, that's your gut telling you that's not what you really want.

✓ ***REALITY CHECK*** When Marianne started junior high, she had a big clique of friends, but she soon got dumped by her old friends, who didn't think she was "cool" enough. "I had to 'shop around' for friends, as absurd as that sounds," she says. "I had a few choices. My best friend from elementary school had a group of friends who were nice enough, but I was a reject so they weren't exactly eager to have me in their group. I could've gone crawling back to my previous group, the 'cool, popular group,' if I seriously committed myself to being popular.

"And thirdly, I could've joined the rejects — the girls who had suffered the same fate as me. We pretty much banded together naturally, but I remember thinking that they were REJECTS, and I was simply not a reject and shouldn't be lumped in a group with other outcasts."

Marianne chose to stick to the group she felt most drawn to naturally — the so-called "rejects" — even though, logically, anyone who cared about being popular wouldn't have done that. She's glad she made the choice she did now: "Through it all, all of us 'rejects' became really close, and we still are. I think I made the right choice — my friends are smart, accepting, and have great futures ahead of them."

5. **How will this choice affect me?** Will you have to do anything special to carry out this option? Will you get in trouble or have to make more choices as a result of it?

✔ ***REALITY CHECK*** Besides feeling drawn to the other "rejects," Marianne also realized that to try to join one of the other groups, she would have to change herself to be accepted. "I would've had to change my whole personality, and I knew that if a group of people demanded that I change for them, they weren't true friends," she says. "Plus, I knew that it would take practically a miracle for a 'cool' clique to accept me, and I didn't want another round of humiliation when I got rejected yet again."

6. **How will this choice affect other people?** Will this option hurt other people or get them in trouble? Will it affect someone else's life in some other way?

If you have a lot of time to make your decision, you can sit down and write through the Choices Checklist.

Another thing you can do is to make a **pros and cons list**. This can help you weigh each possible option logically, especially if neither choice has a higher moral weight (like if you're trying to decide between joining a soccer league or a swim club). Set out one sheet of paper for each option. Write that option at the top of the page. Divide each paper into two columns, one PRO and one CON. Under PRO, write down all the arguments in favor of that choice. Under CON, write down all the arguments against it. (You can use the Choices Checklist to help you come up with reasons.) Do the same for all your options and compare them.

✳***WORK IT!*** Read through the following situations and think about what you would do in each one. What is the right thing to do? Ask your friends what they think and compare and discuss your answers.

1. The night before a huge test, your best friend calls with a crisis — something very emotional but not life threatening. He or she needs to talk, but you need to study. How about if your friend called in the mid-

dle of the season finale of your favorite TV show?

2. Would you rather play a sport (or join some other extracurricular activity) that you were really good at, but you didn't know anyone on the team, or play a sport that you were only so-so at, but all your friends were on the team? Why?

3. During a test, you notice one of your class-mates cheating. What do you do? What if it were a friend of yours? What if it were your best friend? What if you knew that this per-son needed to get a good grade on the test to pass the class?

4. Your grandma gives you thirty dollars for your birthday. You want to use the money to buy a couple of CDs you've been want-ing for a long time, but you know Gran thinks all pop music is evil and wouldn't ap-prove of your purchase. Do you buy the CDs? What if you knew that your grandma would ask you what you bought with the money?

5. Your friends decide to play a prank on a kid you know. You think the prank is kind of mean but also kind of funny. What do you do?

6. You swing by the food court at the mall for a bite to eat. When you sit down with your food, you glance at your receipt and realize that the guy at the cash register undercharged you. Would you go back and point out the mistake?

7. Some kids at school have been harassing one of your friends. Your friend is pretty upset about it but doesn't want to tell her parents. What would you do? What if you were the one who was being harassed?

8. You know your older brother or sister has been sneaking out a lot late at night, but you don't know why. Do you tell your parents? What if you know your sib is sneaking out to meet friends who are definitely up to no good?

9. You want to go for pizza with friends, but you have no money. You see your dad left five dollars on the kitchen table by acci-

dent, and he probably wouldn't miss it. Do you take it? If you do, do you tell him?

10. You've done something wrong. (You decide what that might be — breaking school rules, breaking your parents' rules, whatever you think makes sense.) If you confess, you'll get a bad but not horrible punishment. If you don't confess, you might get away with it — *but* if you get caught, you'll get an even worse punishment than if you had just confessed. Do you confess or keep quiet?

WORK IT! Think of more situations like in the previous exercise, either from real life or made up. A list of these questions makes a thought-provoking game to play at a party or sleepover.

LINKS
If you liked this activity, you might want to check out *The Kids' Book of Questions*, by Gregory Stock. It's full of more make-you-think questions.

You decided. Now what?

Every choice you make has consequences. Sometimes the consequences are good, sometimes they're bad, but no decision is without them. Being independent and mature enough to make your own choices — no matter how big or small those choices are — also means taking responsibility for those choices, no matter what happens.

That might sound a little scary, but it's really not. If you made your decision carefully enough, you probably already thought about at least some of the consequences that might come from it. You should be prepared for those. Taking responsibility for your choices simply means being willing to *own* that choice, to claim it as yours and defend it to everyone else.

> "In the long run we shape our lives and we shape ourselves. The process never ends until we die. And the choices we make are ultimately our own responsibility."
> — Eleanor Roosevelt, U.S. First Lady, author, speaker, activist, diplomat

✓ *REALITY CHECK* In Chapter 2, we talked about Chelsye, who decided to become assistant editor of her school paper. One consequence of this decision was that she couldn't spend as much time on her other activities, but since she had already thought about how to reorganize her priorities, she was prepared for that consequence.

Amy's decision to be part of the "bad" crowd had negative consequences — she broke her parents' rules, and eventually her parents caught and punished her. "I deserved it, too," she says. "Everything I was doing went against my better judgment and my values and everything I had been taught to honor. Getting caught was the best thing that ever could have happened to me."

Taking responsibility for a decision *doesn't* mean you have to stick to it even if it turns out to be wrong. **You always have the right to change your mind, and making mistakes is a part of life.** There's nothing wrong with admitting you made the wrong decision, the way Amy now feels she did.

But you shouldn't abandon a choice you know is right just because it's difficult or unpopular or because other people say you should. **Doing the right thing can sometimes mean going against the crowd.** People will criticize your choices from time to time — there's no way around that. There will be times when you'll have to stick to a choice that lots of people think is wrong or dumb. You may even have to defend your choices to others.

That's when making decisions carefully, according to your values and priorities, really makes a difference. **If you know you made the best decision you could, and you know in your heart it's right for you, then it's a lot easier to stay strong.**

When your decisions are questioned or criticized, ask yourself: Who is criticizing my choice? Is this someone I respect? Does the criticism have any truth to it? If you still feel strongly that you made the right choice, let the critics know: "I see your point, but this is what's right for me." Take pride in being true to yourself — and *your* values — instead of going along with everyone else!

✂•***LINKS***
Flip back to Chapter 2 (What Matters to You — and Why It Matters) to read more about sticking to your values.

✔ ***REALITY CHECK*** Maeve says, "I dress and act differently from most people around me, so people question my choices all the time. At times, you can feel overpowered by these people. When people knock you down, it's hard to get back up. But you must. You have to stay true to yourself."

☀"WORK IT!" Design a flag or banner that symbolizes your pride in your values. (You could also make a flag that symbolizes your background, your achievements, your future, or even a specific choice that you've made.) What shape will it be? What colors will you use, and what do they stand for? What kinds of symbols or designs will you put on it, and what do they mean? After you've come up with a design, make the flag using construction paper or cloth. Use markers, paint, stickers, glitter, or anything else you'd like to decorate it. Choose a spot in your bedroom and hang it with pride!

Chapter Five

Accepting Yourself – and Everyone Else

Loving yourself

As you explore who you are and who you could be, you'll discover all sorts of new things about yourself. Some of them will be easy to love, others you might not be so crazy about. But it's important to embrace *all* the different parts of yourself, old and new, good and not-so-good.

I'm not talking about giving yourself hugs or scribbling "I ♥ ME" all over your notebooks. There might be parts of yourself you feel like changing — there's nothing wrong with that. But for now, those things are a part of who you are, and you wouldn't be complete without them! In fact, once you learn to accept them, some of the things that seemed less lovable can end up being the very things that really make you unique. (For example, I used to hate my crooked front teeth, but now I appreciate them as something special and quirky about my appearance.)

All you need is one thing — anything — that you love about yourself. Sounds corny, but feeling good about just one thing in your life can help remind you of *all* the awesome things there are to love about you.

✔ ***REALITY CHECK*** There are plenty of different things to love about yourself. Christina is proud of how outspoken she is. Izzy says, "I love that I'm funny, because making people laugh is really important." Sydney likes her blue eyes. Courtney says, "I love it that I keep an open mind about things, even when it's hard." Kate is proud of her independence and strength: "I sometimes surprise myself with my titanium core."

WRITE IT! What's something about yourself that you're really proud of? If you already listed things you're proud of in Chapter 3, pick something different. (Check out the lists you made in Chapter 1 for more inspiration.)

✂ ***LINKS***
Flip back to Chapter 1 ("Who Am I?") and Chapter 2 (What Matters to You — and Why It Matters) for more on figuring out the core of the whole you. You'll find more about loving yourself on the outside, from head to toe, in *Body and Mind*, Chapter 1 (Discovering Your Body).

Why are you proud of this? Give an example of a time when that trait was important. (Did your creativity help you come up with great ideas for a school dance? Did your hard work earn you an A on a tough test?)

_____

_____

_____

Like I said before, sometimes there might be things about you that other people don't like — maybe things you're not too crazy about yourself. But acknowledging all those parts of yourself — yes, including the ones that don't seem like your "best" parts — strengthens your sense of self and helps you to know the whole you better. Provided it isn't something destructive (like torturing animals or skipping school), loving — or at least accepting — those less popular parts of yourself can make you feel happier and saner in your whole life. Remember Kate, in Chapter 1, who embraced her geekiness?

✂*LINKS*
Read about Kate and how you can choose the way you see yourself in Chapter 1 ("Who Am I?").

☞ "WRITE IT!" What's something about yourself that you're not so crazy about? Why?

_____

_____

_____

What's a _good_ thing about that not-so-great
characteristic? If you wished that you weren't
so stubborn, can you flip it around and say that
sometimes your stubbornness is good, like
when it gives you the strength to stick to your
beliefs?

_____

_____

_____

"I have confidence in ME!"

When Maria sang those words in the movie _The Sound
of Music_, she was giving herself a lift as she was on
her way to facing a new challenge — becoming a gov-
erness. By reminding herself that she was ready for
anything, she gave herself the strength and courage she
needed to face her new job with confidence.

> "Go confidently in the direction of your dreams! Live the life you've imagined."
> — Henry David Thoreau, author, philosopher, and naturalist

Self-confidence helps you tackle whatever may come your way. When you're confident in yourself and what you can do, you're better able to deal with challenges and difficulties. **Having confidence in who you are helps you stay strong and whole in good times and in bad.** It helps you hold on to what's important to you and allows you to feel proud of yourself when you achieve your goals.

Being confident helps you explore and stretch yourself, too. When you're confident in something you can do well, you can build on those strengths and push yourself even further, do it even better. And you can take that confidence and use it to try new things, knowing that, even if you mess up, you have enough confidence in yourself to try again.

WRITE IT! List five things you're confident you can do. They can be small or large: "I have nice handwriting," "I am a great baby-sitter," "I can run faster than all my friends," "I know how to skate backward," anything you want. If you already listed things that you're proud of in the

previous section or in Chapter 3, you should list
five *new* things this time.

_____

_____

_____

_____

_____

☀*WORK IT!* Pick one of the things from the
previous exercise, and take it to the next level.
So, if you can run faster than all your friends,
can you try to run faster than *you* have ever run
before or join a track team? If you're a good
artist, can you spend more time drawing or
take an art class to learn more? If you're a fast
reader, can you pick out a big, thick classic
book to read? If you're a great baby-
sitter, can you expand the number of
families you sit for?

> **☙*LINKS***
> Knowing who
> you are is the
> first step in feel-
> ing confident
> about yourself.
> Turn to Chapter
> 1 ("Who Am I?")
> for more on
> discovering
> yourself.

If you feel like you could use some
more confidence once in a while, the good
news is that you can always find ways to
build it up. Even people who are naturally

overflowing with confidence occasionally have moments when they'd appreciate a little boost, like when it's time to tackle an especially hard task. So it's good to keep doing things to lift your confidence, just to make sure you stay strong.

> ✔ *REALITY CHECK* To keep her confidence up, Amy focuses on the things she knows she's good at. "I *know* I'm a good writer, and that lets me walk around with the security and confidence I need to be happy," she says. "I'm proud of what I can do and that makes me confident."

One way to keep your self-confidence going strong is through *affirmations*. That's what Maria was doing when she sang "I Have Confidence." (Don't worry, I'm not going to suggest that you sing at the top of your lungs while running through the mountains — chances are you don't have any mountains handy, anyway.) Affirmations work on the principle that, if you tell yourself something enough, sooner or later you'll really believe it. By repeating a confidence-boosting phrase again and again, either out loud or in writing, you'll start to take that phrase to heart. Some examples of affirmations you could do:

I am smart.
I am a creative person.
I am a good writer (or _____).
I am talented at _____.
I feel positive and optimistic.
I am strong and confident.

✳ *WORK IT!* Try doing affirmations. Choose a sentence that you think will help keep you confident. Repeat each affirmation to yourself ten times in a row every day for a week. You can either do this in writing or out loud. (To do it out loud, stand in front of a mirror, look yourself in the eye, and say your affirmations in a strong, confident voice — no whispering or mumbling!) You might feel silly doing this at first — that's okay. If it feels dorky, you're doing it right. Just keep doing it and see how you feel at the end of the week.

✸ *WORK IT!* Give someone else some affirmation. Tell someone you know, in person or in writing, how great he or she is. Be as specific as possible — tell your friend that she's a fantastic artist, tell your dad that you appreciate what a good listener he is, write a note to a former teacher to say how much you liked being in her class, compliment a classmate on a great presentation.

There are lots of other ways you can keep your confidence up or boost it if you ever feel it slipping. Try some of these, or come up with your own.

✓ *REALITY CHECK* "To boost my confidence, I carry around a folded piece of paper in my pocket," says Jeff. "On this paper are two inspirational quotes and a picture of Steve Prefontaine and Lance Armstrong, my role models. When I get down, I'll look at this, read it over a few times, and it gives me a boost."

✳"WORK IT!" Collect inspirational quotes of your own. When you're reading a book or magazine or watching TV, make a note when you come across a passage that you find striking, inspiring, or memorable. If a friend says something particularly wise or you overhear a great line from a stranger, write it down. You can also flip through quotation books — of course, you can start with classics like *Bartlett's Familiar Quotations,* but there are also tons of specialized quote books about sports, love, friendship, and more. Check out the reference section of your local library or bookstore. Or go to Bartleby.com *(http://www.bartleby.com/),* where you can electronically search classic fiction, nonfiction, and reference books for free.

What should you do with these quotes when you find them? I used to copy quotes I loved into a quote journal, but there are tons of other things you can do. Make them into a scroll — write them on a long roll of paper, and add to the scroll as you find new quotes. Copy them onto slips of paper and stick the slips all over your locker or desk, or carry them around in your pocket, like Jeff does. Work them into a collage. You could even write them on your walls, if your parents are really relaxed about that kind of thing. (If they're not, you could make posters instead!)

✳ *WORK IT!* Make yourself a "booster book." Fill a little booklet with things you're proud of — accomplishments, personality traits, anything. (You can buy small blank books with cool covers at most bookstores. Or make your own: Fold over four to five sheets of paper, staple along the crease to make a booklet, or punch two holes along the crease and thread a ribbon through them. Be sure to decorate the cover!) Get creative — write down the things you're proud of, draw them, stick in photos of yourself doing cool things, write in affirmations or other exercises from this chapter, decorate the pages however you like. Add inspirational quotes or anything else that gives you a lift. You can even get your friends to write proud, confidence-boosting messages to you. Keep your booster book in a safe place and look at it whenever you need a boost.

★*WORK IT!* Try these **instant confidence boosters** whenever you need an extra dose of personal power:

Find a personal cheerleader. When you want to pump up your confidence about something, talk to someone who believes in you — a friend, your mom or dad — anyone who you know will say lots of nice, supportive, complimentary things.

Picture it. When you're about to tackle a tough task, close your eyes and visualize yourself successfully doing it, in as much detail as you can. (Trying out for a play? Imagine every gesture you'll make and savor the surge of adrenaline you'll feel when your awesome audition is through. Got a big race? Feel the ground under your feet, the wind in your lungs, or the water that your hands move through.)

Pump yourself up. Do jumping jacks, run in place, dance around the room. Getting your

☆*LINKS*
Turn to *Body
and Mind*,
Chapter 3
(Working It), for
more activities
to keep you
feeling powerful
from head to
toe.

☆*LINKS*
Flip to
Creativity,
Chapter 6 (The
Adventure of
Being You), for
more on con-
quering your
fears.

blood moving energizes you and makes you feel more powerful.

Act confident! Scared to start at a new school, ask for directions, or talk to your crush? Hold your head up and *pretend* you're one hundred percent confident. At the very least, you'll fool everyone else — and you'll probably find your pretend confidence turning into real confidence, too.

Accepting others

When you're secure in who you are and what you believe, you can be open to learning about other people, too — without losing your own values. As you know, the world is full of people who are different from you in personality, background, interests, values, you name it. Being open to those differences, and learning to accept them even if you don't like them, helps you explore parts of life that you might not have seen on your own.

✓ ***REALITY CHECK*** Marianne has an open-minded perspective on getting along with dif-

124

ferent kinds of people. "I find it fascinating how people can be so different from myself and each other, and whenever I meet someone drastically different from me I'm curious to learn more about them. One of my friends has this great living room carpeted in red, with white and black leather couches and statues of the Hindu elephant god all over the room — her mom collects them. I think it's so interesting how her house and family are really different from mine. I love noticing all the things that make people different, even little things like their mannerisms, their accents, their clothes, and the things they talk about in everyday conversation."

It can be fun to learn about the ways in which someone is different from you, and discovering those differences can even help you explore new parts of yourself. I'm kind of shy and retiring by nature, but I've always had a few friends who are more daring and wild than I am. Take my friend Cindy, my roommate at music camp two years in a row, who was as outgoing and outspoken as they come. Even though I knew I'd never be as crazy as she was (she used to sneak out of our room after curfew and tell off the counselors when they ticked her off), hanging out with her and being open-minded about her craziness helped me tap into a more outgoing side of myself.

While it's important to be open and explore new things, it's also important to do so without losing sight of the things that are fundamental to you. Cindy taught me about being braver, but I didn't let go of my fundamental values in the process. For example, I knew I wouldn't tell off the counselors like Cindy did, because being respectful to people like counselors and teachers was an important value to me.

There were other girls at camp who couldn't stand Cindy, who thought she was obnoxious. Those girls were quiet and laid back, more like me — I was friends with most of them, too. I think it made them really uncomfortable to be around people who were really different from them. It would have been easy for me to ally myself with them, to decide that, since Cindy and I were so different, we weren't meant to be friends. But by accepting her for who she was and not trying to change her, I learned a lot more about myself and had a lot more fun, too.

✴️*WORK IT!* Head to the library and pick out a book about someone your age who has grown up in a completely different place from you. If you live in the city, you could read about someone who lives on a farm. If you were born in the United States, you could choose a book about a kid from another country. Ask your teacher or librarian for suggestions of good books to choose, or start with the Recommended Reading section in the back of this book.

> **✂️*LINKS***
> *Creativity,* **Chapter 5 (Curiosity Counts), has more on being open to new adventures and ideas. To get the scoop on being accepted** *by* **others, turn to** *Friends and Family,* **Chapter 3 (Fitting In). You can also read about how friendships can add to the whole you in** *Friends and Family,* **Chapter 2 (Friendship).**

Everyone has something to teach us, so learning to accept different kinds of people helps you explore both the world and yourself. People from different cultural backgrounds or with different values can teach you different ways of thinking about the world. Trying to understand why someone acts or dresses a certain way can make you think about why you act or dress the way *you* do. (That kid with the freakish 1980s hairdo? Maybe he doesn't care about trends, or maybe he genuinely likes the '80s.)

Even the most annoying, awful people can teach you something, even if it just shows you what you *don't* want to be. For example, whenever I see someone being mean and nasty to a waitress or a salesclerk at a store, it reminds me that I don't ever want to act that way. Thinking about what makes those people the way they are makes me more aware of why I treat other people the way I do and reinforces my own values.

✓ ***REALITY CHECK*** "A lot of people are genuinely afraid of people different from them and that kind of person I have trouble getting along with," admits Marianne. "Also, some people's personalities just naturally clash — that can't be avoided. My mom and I have really different personalities, and we have plenty of disagreements. But we have a lot of respect for each other's opinions, so everything works out all right." One other bit of wisdom Marianne lives by: "If you're nice to someone, even if it's someone you hate, they will probably be nice back; and if they're not, then they're losers!"

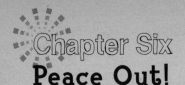

Chapter Six
Peace Out!

Finding inner peace

Do the words "inner peace" conjure up an image of a bald guy in a robe meditating on top of a mountain? Don't worry, I'm not going to ask you to shave your head and give away all your CDs. You've got inner peace already — we're just going to tap into it. No rock climbing required, I swear.

Being at peace is about more than just chilling out. When you're at peace, your spirit feels not only calm and still, but also balanced and content. Maintaining a sense of peacefulness is crucial to wholeness, because it's hard to feel free to explore yourself when you're agitated or stressed or feeling disrupted inside. When you let yourself be calm and peaceful, mentally *and* physically, you gain perspective on your whole life and self. It works the other way, too — **the more whole you feel, the more at peace you'll be.**

You probably have things you do when you want to relax or quiet your brain, places you like to go when you want to feel calm and cozy. If so, you've already

THE WHOLE YOU: SPIRIT

found ways to maintain a sense of inner peace. We'll be exploring different ways you can find peace, from taking care of your inner spirit to looking on the bright side of life.

✔ ***REALITY CHECK*** How do you find peace? "When no one's home, I get in the bathtub and sing really loudly," says Izzy. Shauna finds peace at church: "Even if it's boring, you always feel good afterward," she says. Sydney likes hanging out with her dog when she needs to chill out. "Music and writing make me feel peaceful — when I'm writing a story while listening to music, that's when I'm at my best," says Chelsye. "Being with people who love me makes me feel peaceful as well."

WRITE IT! What makes you feel peaceful? Write down ten things. They can be anything that soothes your spirit, like curling up under your comforter when it's cold out, watching the clouds go by, listening to your favorite CD, taking a long bath, watching your dog napping. Ask friends and family to make their own lists, and compare.

_____

_____

_____

_____

_____

_____

_____

_____

_____

_____

☀ *WORK IT!* *Meditation* is a way of focusing your mind and clearing your head of all the extra clutter, so you can relax. For thousands of years, people have used meditation to calm their spirits. Like I said, you don't need to climb a mountain or become a monk here. Try these simple meditation exercises to help you feel peaceful.

Listen to yourself. Sit or lie in a comfortable position. Close your eyes and breathe deeply

"You do not need to leave your room. Remain sitting at your table and listen. Do not even listen, simply wait. Do not even wait, be quite still and solitary. The world will freely offer itself to you to be unmasked, it has no choice, it will roll in ecstasy at your feet."
— Franz Kafka, author

in and out through your nose. Let your body relax. Feel all your muscles loosening and softening. Focus on the air flowing in through your nose, filling your lungs, and expanding your chest and belly, then flowing out again. Concentrating on your breathing like this clears your head of other thoughts and lets your mind quiet down. (If you like, have someone slowly and quietly read these instructions to you, so you don't have to try to memorize them.) Careful — if you do this close to bedtime, you might get so relaxed you fall asleep!

Write it out. Grab two sheets of paper and a pen or pencil. Start writing as fast as you can, anything that comes to mind — if you can't think of anything, just keep writing "I can't think of anything" until something comes into your head. Let the words flow out — emptying random junk out of your head and onto paper is another way to meditate. Don't stop until you've covered both sheets of paper, front and back.

Nourishing the spirit

Nourishing your spirit is another impor-tant way to maintain inner peace and bal-ance. It simply means doing things that refresh you from the inside, so you have more energy to deal with life and can enjoy every day more. The same way you eat to nourish your body — **your spirit needs to be fed, too!**

Anything that rejuvenates you mentally or emo-tionally counts as nourishing the spirit — taking a long walk, reading a good book, picking flowers, and espe-cially really selfish, just-for-me things like buying your-self your favorite candy or taking a long bubble bath. Taking care of your spirit and doing nice things for yourself (and other people!) not only gives you com-fort, it inspires and energizes you.

It's good to make a point of recharging yourself regularly, just to maintain your strength of spirit. But it's especially important to take care of yourself when you feel stressed or sad — times like that are like run-

LINKS
Get inspiration about other ways to write your way to peace in *Creativity*, Chapter 3 (Write On).

ning a marathon for your spirit. By giving yourself a little extra TLC, you'll make sure that you have plenty of inner fuel to tackle whatever comes your way.

✔ ***REALITY CHECK*** "When I need to recharge I just run," says Cricket. "I know, running when you're tired sounds weird. But it helps me organize and reenergize. I run in the woods, because it's so peaceful — and there are no cars to hit you!"

WRITE IT! Make a list of 10 totally selfish things that you like to do and that make you happy — hiding out and reading all weekend, playing video games, rubbing your feet, sunbathing, playing with your old toys, whatever you want.

✄***LINKS***
You'll find tips on managing stress in *Body and Mind,* Chapter 4 (Feed Your Brain). (*Body and Mind* also has lots more on fueling your body and brain in general.) Dealing with your emotions can also help you find peace — you can read about that in Chapter 3 (The Way You Feel).

_____

_____

_____

_____

_____

Next time you feel overwhelmed or stressed or just feel like being good to yourself, pick something from your list and do it!

Having a place to call your own helps a lot when you need to feed your spirit or find peace. It's hard to relax or really feel like you're taking care of yourself if you never have any privacy or if you feel like you don't have anywhere special to get away from other people. Plus, when you have a place that's all your own, just being in that place can be rejuvenating for you.

WORK IT! Create a space that's just for you, whether it's your whole bedroom, a corner of a room you share, even a tree house or a piece of your backyard. This should be a place where you can have privacy, keep personal objects, and just sit, relax, and feel safe. Decorate

> "There is no need to go to India or anywhere else to find peace. You will find that deep place of silence right in your room, your garden, or even your bathtub."
> — Elisabeth Kübler-Ross, psychiatrist

your space with things that make you feel peaceful and good inside, whether that means hanging pictures of people or places you love, displaying a special collection or other objects that are important to you, using soothing colors or fabrics — whatever makes you feel good. Make sure everyone knows it's *your* space.

☀*WORK IT!* Design the inside of your very own dream house, with rooms and spaces for all the things that are important to you. Is catching up with your friends a top priority? Maybe your dream house will include a big room used just for sleepovers, or a communications center with a fast Internet connection and your own phone line. Is writing or reading one of your favorite things? Maybe your house will have a beautiful library, a special writing desk, or a big comfy chair perfect for reading in. Like to have your privacy? Add a super-secret tower room, that only you have the key for. Don't forget to include spaces for the people or pets that live with you. You could even design a special guest room just for your grandma or your best friend. Go crazy! Your dream house doesn't have to be realistic, it only has to be fun.

Faith

The word "faith" is often associated with religion, and religion helps lots of people find inner peace. One very simple way it does that is through the particular rituals and beliefs of whatever religion you're a part of. Praying, meditating, singing hymns, or taking part in other rites and rituals of your religion are all ways to calm your spirit. The rituals themselves are often soothing, and the beliefs behind these rituals help nurture your spirit and give you a sense of belonging, community, and peace.

More important, **having faith means believing in something outside of yourself,** whether it's God, an Earth Mother, or the creative flow of the universe. Every religion has a set of beliefs that helps define our purpose, the meaning of our lives. Seeing the big picture this way, and having

> **✂ *LINKS***
> For more on how your connections to other people (from your religious community to your friends and family) make you whole, pick up *Friends and Family*.

"Faith is the bird that feels the light and sings when the dawn is still dark."
— Rabindranath Tagore, author

a sense of where you fit into it, can put life and all its pesky problems into perspective. It helps you have a greater sense of harmony within yourself, even when the world around you doesn't feel all that harmonious.

Faith isn't only about religion, though. You can also find faith and perspective in other things outside yourself — like a community or a nonreligious philosophy or set of values. You can have faith in positive thinking, in science, or in anything that matters to you. Maybe you have faith in your parents or faith that things will always turn out for the best. No matter what you believe in, faith anchors your spirit and gives it strength.

✂°*LINKS*
To think about how faith fits into *your* big picture, turn to Chapter 2 (What Matters to You — and Why It Matters).

✓ *REALITY CHECK* Shauna is Catholic, and her religion plays a big role in her life. She believes in heaven and other Christian concepts, and she goes to church every week. "In church, you try to talk to God, and sometimes I feel like I really am," she says. Other institutions in her religion are important to her, too: "I like confession, because you can say anything."

▶"WRITE IT!" What do you believe in? Write your own statement of belief. It can be based on religious beliefs, or it can be something as basic as "I believe the universe is basically a good place" or "I believe that love can conquer any problem."

> "I believe. I believe. It's silly, but I believe."
> — Susan (played by Natalie Wood) in *Miracle on 34th Street*

_____

_____

_____

Looking on the bright side

Another way to find perspective and peace is through *optimism*. Optimism means taking a positive view of life: expecting that things will generally turn out for the best, or focusing on the positive side of a situation. Its opposite — pessimism — means taking a negative view of the world. The most extreme pessimists expect nothing but the worst out of life. They expect that the world is against them, that they will always lose, and that only bad things can happen. As you might guess, it's pretty hard to be at peace with yourself or with life if you feel this way — and it's not much fun to be around, either!

Now, it's not realistic to have a totally sunny view of absolutely everything all the time. Bad things do happen, and sometimes people are mean and life isn't fair. And remember, back in Chapter 3, I said you should never, ever push away bad feelings and pretend they're not happening. Letting yourself get upset or feel sad is normal — heck, it's *important* to recognize when you feel lousy.

> **Did you know?** People who are optimists tend to be healthier than people who are pessimists.

But **having a positive attitude in the face of life's challenges, and having faith that everything will turn out okay in the end, can help you feel more at peace about life overall.** This is especially helpful when you're upset or feeling down — if you believe that things will get better, it's a lot easier to get through the tough times and to motivate yourself to do whatever it takes to *make* things better. And even when things are just fine, believing that they can get even better, and focusing on the good things that happen instead of the bad,

> **"Optimism is the faith that leads to achievement. Nothing can be done without hope and confidence."** — Helen Keller, author and lecturer

makes you feel more hopeful and excited to explore everything that's out there.

°°°*LINKS*
Chapter 5
(Accepting
Yourself — and
Everyone Else)
talks about how
being optimistic
about *yourself*
is a huge
source of
power. Feeling
optimistic about
the future? Go
to *Creativity*,
Chapter 7
(Dreaming and
Doing), to read
about setting
your sights high
and going for
your dreams.

WRITE IT! **Quiz: Are you an optimist?**

Do you look on the bright side, or are you a more grumbly type? Take this quiz and find out.

1. You've just had the worst day ever — you know, slept late, hair looks funny, said something stupid in class, tripped in the hall when everyone was looking, dropped your homework in a puddle, fought with your friends, fought with your parents, Brussels sprouts for dinner, that kind of day. How do you feel?
   a. Like nothing will ever go right again.
   b. Pretty yucky, but you'll get over it . . . eventually.
   c. Fine — you're focusing on how much better tomorrow will be.

2. You studied really hard for a big test, hoping to get an A or at least a B. Instead, you got a D. What do you do?

   a. Talk to your teacher to try to figure out what went wrong and how you can be better prepared for the next test. You know you can do better next time!

   b. Maybe get a tutor, but don't knock yourself out — how much harder could you really study?

   c. What's the point? Obviously, you just don't have what it takes to do well in this class.

3. A girl in your class is having a party in two weeks, and you're the only one of your friends who hasn't been invited. What do you think?

   a. I'll check with my friends to see if they know why I wasn't invited.

   b. She probably hates me — that's why I wasn't invited. I don't care — I hate her, too.

   c. Maybe she just forgot to invite me — I'll ask her.

For numbers 4 to 8, circle whether you disagree, sort of agree, or totally agree with each statement.

4. I usually assume that most people are basically good at heart.

   disagree   sort of agree   totally agree

5. If I really put my mind to it, I can do just about anything I want.

   disagree   sort of agree   totally agree

6. It's up to me whether or not I succeed in life.

   disagree   sort of agree   totally agree

7. I feel hopeful about life most of the time.

   disagree   sort of agree   totally agree

8. I feel excited when I look forward to the future.

   disagree   sort of agree   totally agree

19–24 points: You've got a sunny view of the world in general and when things go wrong, you always look on the bright side or try to figure out how you can make things better. Keep it up! If you scored on the high end of this category (23 or 24 points), just make sure that your bright outlook doesn't blind you to when people are really treating you badly.

SCORING:
1. a=1, b=2, c=3
2. a=3, b=2, c=1
3. a=2, b=1, c=3
4–8. Give yourself 1 point for every "disagree," 2 points for every "sort of agree," and 3 points for every "totally agree."

13–18 points: You're fairly optimistic about life, and you maintain a positive attitude most of the time. At the same time, you've got a realistic streak that keeps you from being totally starry-eyed. When you do find yourself slipping into a pessimistic point of view, try boosting yourself with exercises like the one after this quiz.

8–12 points: Why the long face? Life isn't as bad as all that, you know. To boost your optimism, start small — try thinking about something good in your life, no matter how little it is, and focusing on that whenever you're feeling pessimistic or grouchy. (The next section has more on being thankful for the good things in your life.) If you scored really low in this range (like 8 to 9 points), or if you find yourself unable to think positively at all, you may be depressed — please check out the link to the left.

> ✂ *LINKS*
> If you're having a tough time feeling optimistic about anything, turn to *Body and Mind,* Chapter 5 (Feeling Healthy), for more on dealing when life is the pits.

☀"WORK IT!" On a separate sheet of paper, write about or draw something that happened today from a pessimistic point of view. ("School stunk. It was raining, so my shoes got wet, and we couldn't go outside. There was a pop quiz in social studies and I had a really hard time. . . .") Then write or draw it from an optimistic point of view. ("The rain looked cool beating against the windows in Ms. Vanderpool's class. It felt really cozy to be inside listening to the rain. The pop quiz was hard, but I was surprised how much I knew without studying. . . .")

What are you thankful for?

Like optimism, being grateful for what you have helps you keep your whole life in perspective. By thinking of the things you're thankful for, you remind yourself of the positive parts of your life. You can take comfort in the good things, no matter how crazy or awful one day may be. And if you do have a bad day, being thankful for the good stuff reminds you that life is more than just one awful day — and the whole you is more than

145

just these yucky feelings. There's a reason why we have a whole holiday dedicated to giving thanks!

✓ ***REALITY CHECK*** There are countless things to be thankful for in life, big or small. T.J. says he's thankful for "every experience I have ever had." Chelsye says, "I am most thankful for my mother. She is my true best friend and I would do anything for her." "I'm happy that braces look good on me!" Shauna says. And Amy jokes that she's thankful for "clams, wool socks, Cheez-Its, Fresca, Q-tips, cars, boys . . ."

WRITE IT! List 10 things you're thankful for in your life right now. Some examples: grilled cheese sandwiches, friends, your favorite teacher.

_____

_____

_____

_____

_____

_____

_____

_____

_____

_____

✳*WORK IT!* Every night for the next month, write down three things that made you happy that day, even if they were really small. (You can keep your lists in a notebook and turn it into a "gratitude journal.") Forcing yourself to find positive things to remember and be thankful for gets you to put even the crummiest day in perspective — and helps you celebrate the great days!

✂*LINKS* Find more cool journal ideas in *Creativity,* Chapter 3 (Write On).

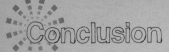

Conclusion
Keeping Your Spirit Alive

Just the first step . . .

Throughout this book, you've been discovering your inner self, strengthening your core values, and getting to know the whole you in different ways. I hope this is only the first step. Exploring your spirit is a journey that will continue throughout your life. By arming yourself with the tools you need to examine your values, set priorities, deal with your feelings, make choices, stay centered, and, most of all, know who you are deep down, you'll make that journey all the more rewarding.

> "What lies behind us and what lies before us are tiny matters, compared to what lies within us."
> — Ralph Waldo Emerson, philosopher, essayist, and poet

Whether you realize it or not, you're adding pieces to the whole you every day. Everything that happens to you, good or bad, can teach you something about yourself and your spirit. And throughout your whole life, as you add to and strengthen your spirit even more, you'll be able to draw on that inner strength and knowledge of yourself to stay whole.

The one and only you

A lot of this book has been pretty serious, but the most important thing I hope you take away from it is a sense of excitement and fun — about yourself! After all, there never has been, and there never will be again, a person with the exact same combination of genes and personality and family and friends and hopes and dreams as you. How fascinating is that?

> **"I celebrate myself, and sing myself."**
> — Walt Whitman, poet

WORK IT! Write your full name (first, middle, last) down the side of a piece of paper. For each letter, think of an adjective or a descriptive phrase that fits you, like this:

Always unusual

Daring

Altruistic

Mushy (in secret)

LINKS
Check back to Chapter 1 ("Who Am I?") for inspiration and reminders of words and phrases you can use.

The result is a unique description of the unique person that is you. When you're done, you can copy the whole thing onto a large piece of construction paper or poster board, using different colors of markers or paints. Decorate your name board and display it proudly. (A name board like this also makes a great present for a friend, sibling, or parent — using the recipient's name, of course!)

"Be really whole and all things will come to you."
— Lao-Tzu, philosopher

So honor the uniqueness of your spirit, and let your individuality shine through! Every little beautiful, crazy, weird part of you is important to cele- brate — because it all comes together to create THE WHOLE YOU.

Recommended Reading

The following is a list of books you might want to check out if you're interested in further exploring some of the themes in this book. There are even some books by and about some of the people I've quoted throughout this book. All of them deal with issues such as values, emotions, and the process of discovering who you are deep down. But, of course, most of all they're just really great reads. I've included books that are recommended for all different ages; check with your teacher or librarian if you have questions about any of them.

FICTION
Sounder, by William Howard Armstrong
The True Adventures of Charlotte Doyle, by Avi
Are You There, God? It's Me, Margaret, by Judy Blume
Summer of the Swans, by Betsy Byars
Walk Two Moons, by Sharon Creech
The Midwife's Apprentice, by Karen Cushman
The Cat Ate My Gymsuit, by Paula Danziger

Julie of the Wolves, by Jean Craighead George

Deliver Us from Evie, by M.E. Kerr

California Blue, by David Klass

To Kill a Mockingbird, by Harper Lee

A Wrinkle in Time, by Madeleine L'Engle

Ella Enchanted, by Gail Carson Levine

The Witch of Blackbird Pond, by Elizabeth George Speare

BIOGRAPHY/AUTOBIOGRAPHY

The Diary of a Young Girl, by Anne Frank

The Story of My Life, by Helen Keller

The Life and Words of Martin Luther King Jr., by Ira Peck

Eleanor Roosevelt: A Life of Discovery, by Russell Freedman

POETRY

I'm nobody! Who are you? by Emily Dickinson (Scholastic Classics edition)

Walt Whitman: Poetry for Young People, by Walt Whitman

About the Author

Jeannie Kim spent the first seventeen years of her life in Wisconsin, but she still hates cold weather. A former editor at *YM* and *Twist,* she is now a full-time writer. Her work has appeared in *CosmoGIRL!,* Tigerbeat.com, and *Your Prom,* as well as many magazines for grownups. In her spare time, she likes to pretend she's a rock star. She lives in New York City with her husband and their cat, Deirdre.